On Trying to Become
a French Paysan

On Trying to Become a French Paysan

and peasant recipes

GARRY HOLDING

Typeset in Quadraat by MacGuru Ltd

ISBN 9782955855607

Printed and bound in Great Britain by Clays Ltd, St Ives plc

Contents

APPENDICES

Acknowledgements

I wish to thank Tom Cross for the beautiful cover illustration and for his line drawings, Stephen Brough for his help and advice and so many friends for their encouragement.

Extracts from « La Vie » magazine are included with the permission of the « Le Monde » Group.

I dedicate the book to Sue, my wife, and our three children – Natalie, Justin and Richard – fellow adventurers.

This is our story.

PART ONE

1

The Quandry

It is often said that everyone in France today who does not actually live in the countryside seems to be related in some way or is friends with someone who does. Consequently, many city dwellers own a 'pied à terre', or a 'maison secondaire' or just part of a property obtained through 'un heritage' when a member of the family died, and practically the whole of the French urban population has some sort of tie or feeling of empathy with fellow compatriots who have the good fortune to 'vivre à la campagne'.

French townspeople, then, do not feel sorry for the poor 'paysan' and some are even jealous of the luxury he enjoys through living to the full his rural life! In France, town and country are still not so divorced as in the UK. This feeling of contentment experienced through living close to the land; this happiness envied by others, of living a simple life is what attracted my wife, Sue, and I some 27 years ago and made us wonder if a French 'paysan' might not just be happier and feel more fulfilled than a teacher and his family living a middle-class life under Maggie Thatcher's policies in GB! I use the word 'paysan' rather than the English word 'peasant' as the latter can be used as a derogatory term – someone uncouth or uncivilised who has an unenviable, hard life, whereas the French equivalent of the word is much more positive; a farmer, a Countryman.

Like so many other Brits, we had for years holidayed in France as a family, motoring and camping here and there, enjoying exploring the 'paysage', 'la gastronomie', 'le doux climat' and the leisurely pace of life; and all of this was way before 'A Year in Provence' and the onslaught of TV programmes highlighting the benefits of moving to France. Gradually, in Sue's thinking and in my own, we wondered if we shouldn't take the risk of crossing the Rubicon and burning our bridges... Very interested in living off the land as far as possible ever since we had devoured John Seymour's book 'Practical Self-Sufficiency' in the late 1970's and had enjoyed the

4

'Good Life' series on television, we had managed to buy a small fell farm at auction and on our 20 acres in West Cumbria we milked our two cows for our dairy needs, reared a couple of pigs every six months and a couple of calves each year, kept hens, ducks, turkeys and geese, produced our own honey, cut our own hay and ate our own garden produce. Sue was the full-time farmer also bringing-up three children whilst I was the farmer's husband, keeping down a very full-time job as a busy music teacher in the local comprehensive community school with my share of farm work at the weekend. A great life, but... When, for the second year running, our hay crop rotted in the field before we could gather it in owing to the constant rain and the 'Soil Association' refused to register our land as being organic because of our proximity to the Sellafield nuclear plant, we decided to sell, take up the offer of a Deputy Headship, live a townie life and 'test' our increasingly strong desire to try self-sufficiency in kinder climes sometime in the future – in France? – by living a more 'normal' life in a country town in County Durham.

The test worked in that we immediately missed living close to the land and of not being in complete control of what we ate and where it came from, and whilst I enjoyed the challenge of my new found role of Second Master and professional development officer in a very reactionary, backward-looking grammar school recently turned comprehensive, after four years of struggling to respond positively to the seemingly endless governmental initiatives we'd had enough. The desire to seek a headship dissipated during yet another trip to France during the Summer of 1988 and we tentatively started to look at the property market with the firm idea of seeing if we could justify taking our eventual dream one step further by buying a spot in 'la belle campagne française'. Our VW camper van took us on a grand tour. Normandy, we found, had a similar climate to that of the UK, Alsace didn't seem to know if it was German or French, the Alpine region was too expensive, Provence was too hot and the Massif Central had very cold winters we were told; we didn't get to the Pyrenees and so we ended-up in an area which we didn't know at all – Poitou-Charentes.

We knew the Dordogne was just to the south and we knew it to be very beautiful but we didn't want to settle in an area that was reputed to be 'Little England' and as there didn't seem to be any Brits in the triangle between Poitiers, Niort and Angoulême we hunted there.

We went into one notaire's office in Sauzé-Vaussais, a small market town and asked if there were any properties for sale – there were very few Estate Agents in those days – and we were handed three very large ring binders with details of dozens of properties which had been 'sur le marché' for several years. The fact that there were so many actually confused us as we were also told that properties rarely sold because potential vendors were reluctant to see their property go! The 'notaire' informed us that property with a bit of land might be advertised as being for sale but as land wasn't being made any more, once it was sold it was gone for ever; it was what had been handed-down and should really go to 'quelqu'un dans la famille'. 'La terre c'est la richesse, et la richesse n'a pas de prix!' Which is it better to have? a few thousand francs (it's soon spent!) or a nice little house with land and all its potential?" Time and time again over the years since then we have been reminded of this contradiction – for instance, when we did choose a property it had been 'on the market' for over 16 years but was now only really for sale because the proprietor – an elderly lady who had lived there as a child before she had eloped with the farm labourer many years before (!) – had lived all her married life in another farm for which she and her husband now wanted some money to be able to modernise another house they had inherited for their old age. Once the sale had been completed we were treated to a memorable meal at which occasion we gave the lady of the house a large box of chocolates; her reaction was that she could never bring herself to eat them as each chocolate repre-sented a stone of the house she had sold us...! We felt as though we had tricked her into selling and even today, after 27 years of living here and after having asked many times, we have only recently been able to buy a tiny piece of land which gives us easier access to our property. The owner didn't use it in any way and we were always allowed to use it and do what we wanted with it – 'servez-vous, faites comme vous voulez' – except buy it! The property we eventually opted for didn't actually figure in any file or in any window-display but one Monday morning, after we had been visiting some friends' property in the Charente who hadn't yet moved in, I was looking in the window of a rare 'Agence Immobilière' only to be literally pulled-into the office by the lady estate agent! When Sue came along, having popped into a shop next door, our 12 year old daughter, Natalie, told her 'Dad's just gone into the house shop' and as soon as Sue crossed the threshold of the agency we were both jostled out by 'Madame' who jumped into the front passenger seat of the VW camper, pushing Sue and the children into the back, saying 'je vais vous montrer quelque chose' How could we resist? And 20 minutes later we had crossed the border into another county, Deux-Sèvres and we were facing what was to become our future home.

This highly persuasive and seemingly very friendly agent (she flattered us by saying how wonderful it was to meet English people who could speak French and because we were so 'sympa' she could arrange for the house to be re-roofed expertly and cheaply...) unfortunately turned-out to be quite dishonest as she convinced us that we should pay the asking price but minus a certain sum which should figure on two separate cheques which she would then give to the vendor separately in cash; this, she told us was traditional practice in France (and it was true that we had heard and read of this quite often in the past'). We were – (eventually) – however, not taken-in by this illegal practice of a 'sous-table' and whilst she tried to keep us from meeting the vendor, saying that she was very old and doddery and not easy to communicate with, that she didn't really want to sell and it was only thanks to her acumen as an estate agent that we could actually buy, when we did meet the vendor and her husband on the day of the signing in the notaire's office, to Madame's chagrin, we actually got on very well and we were invited to that memorable meal.

Facing our future home, then, we found we were in a hamlet which consisted of three houses which were permanently lived-in by French people, two French-owned holiday homes and one English, two uninhabited houses which were semi-derelict and a dozen or so partially ruined houses and barns. Extensive chestnut forests were just 500 metres away with fields of wheat, maize, sunflowers and rapeseed around. The next hamlet was

1 kilometre away and the nearest town 5kms. This was an idyll for us – especially as the hamlet was called 'Le Sauvage' or 'Les Sauvages', depending on which map was consulted; so, accordingly, was this 'the Wilderness' or where 'the Savages' lived?! Whichever, we loved it and could see potential...but exactly what would we be getting for 16u (160 ooofrs or £16,000)? And who would be our neighbours? What would they think of us? Would they accept us? What would we have to do in order to be able to integrate? What were the winters like? Could we make our dream come true, and at what cost; What about the children? Did I really want to give up a good income and risk all in a foreign country...? Lots of things to mull over in the camper van that night. Obviously, we had constantly thought about all of this before we'd come to France but when you're actually faced with a property within your grasp it takes a lot of courage to actually take the plunge! Most of our friends in the UK had declared us as being either very brave or very stupid to even think of embarking on such a project.

The biggest question to answer was centred on income and the standard of living when bringing up children. Whilst Sue and I were happy with what 'living off the land' meant, our 6, 11 and 12 year old children who loved the countryside as they had always lived close to, if not actually in the country, had also become used to living a comfortable middle-class life. After paying off the UK mortgage, buying our French home and paying for the move there would be little left for meeting renovation costs beyond roof and sanitation, buying stock, etc.

Of course, we knew there would be hardly any employment opportunities for supplementary income as the area we had chosen was one of desertification where small farms were being absorbed into bigger ones – something which had begun years before, even if this was happening some forty years after it had happened in the UK. All of the remaining farmsteads still seemed to be very small and they didn't give the impression of being efficient but while they might not have been making much money they did contribute to feeding the nation and the locals did seem to be happy and friendly towards us! The four nearest County towns where one might find employment were all some 60kms away but we didn't want to come to France to join those town-dwellers who understood the quality of life that living 'à la campagne' had to offer yet had to work 'en ville' and consequently lead a stressful life! (A recent survey found that there were 14 million gardeners in France out of a population of 65 million and that of those who were not, 50% would like to have a 'potager' (they had been 30% in 2008)).

After our night of excited discussions in the VW van Sue and I had made our minds up – and the children had been caught-up in the excitement which their parents were exuding! We would buy the le Sauvage property, sell-up in England and rent for a year there with the intention of having basic repairs done to the French property before moving piecemeal to France if all 'went well' or, if not, keep it as a holiday home to perhaps retire to when the time came. We were absolutely sure that, as a family, we would be happier in France by going back to the land and living in an environment where simple things were more satisfying. We felt that if we prepared the children well enough over the year we could ensure that making the move from one culture to another – or, adding a second culture to the one they had been brought-up in – could only be enriching for them and would hold them in good stead in the Europe of the future. This was to be our Family Adventure, but first we needed to examine the property thoroughly and meet the neighbours...

2

The Dream House

Our future home was, like all of the other properties in the 'hameau', built out of limestone which had been quarried from a field ('Les Chailles' – slang for stones) just 200 metres down the road with red mud being used as mortar and was roofed with red and yellow Roman tiles – 'courantes' sitting underneath 'les châpeaux' top tiles which had been manufactured at the 'tuilerie' 4kms down the road. The main building of house, stable, barn and cowshed with granary above was South-facing. At right-angles to one side was a handsome pigsty with another barn with calf pens a bit further away and another low building opposite which had been used for poultry, with the traditional wooden single toilet structure in a small orchard some 30 metres away from the house door. The ensemble made for an enclosed, grassed yard.

Facing the main house we could see large stones sticking out of the two sides of the right-hand gable-end and just one metre away was a single roomed cottage in the corner of the yard which seemed to be much older than the main farm house. We were informed by the vendor that the house itself had been built in about 1850 and the stones left sticking-out were to facilitate an extension to the house which would have meant knocking the cottage down. When the vendor's father had wanted to do just this, his mother-in-law's mother, whose home it was, had refused to move out. This was where she had brought-up 4 children – in one room! – and this was where she would stay; so the stones remain there today – and we could see a good use for that tiny cottage! Behind the pigsty was another long building, at right angles to the main house, in which there was another 2-roomed cottage facing our way and with two houses and two barns facing in the other direction – a back-to-back terrace! The cottage facing our way, very derelict, was also in our lot but the rest of the terrace, even more derelict, belonged to an old bachelor who had acquired it some 20 years before but who had abandoned it – except for the garden which was in a very fine state indeed. We learned from this 'neighbour' that our vendor's father had owned the small cottage and that his brother had owned the other side but that the two brothers had not spoken to each other for years because their wives had fallen out! Sadly, they had died without making-up, with the surviving brother even refusing to attend the other's funeral... We explored our 'dream house' but there wasn't much to see! It consisted of one square room, about 25sq.m with quite a high ceiling, whitewashed walls and chestnut floorboards except for two small areas – one in front of the fireplace and one in the sink area – which were of stone. In one corner, against the wall, was a 'lit bâteau' or 'lit à rouleaux' – a narrow double bed with waist-high headboard and bottom board topped with a round pole. Typical of the area, it was made of very solid oak and ornately carved on the side facing the room. There was a curtain hanging from the 'marquise' above which could be drawn around the bed for more privacy. Our vendor, as a child had slept in another corner of this one room.

In the corner diagonally opposite was the 'sink' – a large slab of stone, slightly indented and angled so that water would run towards the wall and out of a hole directly onto the roots of the vine planted just outside; the vine which was trained along the whole of the front of the house – 'la treille'.

The sink was not deep enough to hold any water

and instead, a bucket or basin was set upon it. At face height was a small oval hole which gave a bit of light and through which one could spy out. This was called 'l'oeil du bac' and can be seen in every house around. Of course we were excited about having a vine growing up the front wall of the house but the owner eventually told us that it was a variety which was now considered as being illegal ('ça fait du vin qui rend fou'!). She did, however, make pineau – the local aperitif – out of it, which we had the pleasure of tasting at the 'memorable meal'. Cooking was done on the open fire where only wood was burned. Dog irons, trivet and a large pot hung from an adjustable ratchet ('crêmaillère') made up the basic cooking equipment. Elsewhere in the village, in some houses, in addition to the open hearth there was 'un potager' which was a piece of equipment built into one of the walls some 90cm from the ground. It consisted of a square hole into which hot embers could be placed with a grill just above on which a cooking pot could be placed with the whole of the potager enclosed in a cupboard with slatted doors. In this way food could be left to cook slowly whilst work was being done in the fields. There wasn't a cellar but the 'cave' was on the north wall of the house where large wine barrels were stored and there was a 'garde-manger' (larder) also on the north wall where food was stored. The large table was situated squarely in the middle of the room. Above this the only electric bulb in the room hung. Previously, before electricity, there would have been a suspended rack here in which would have been placed one plate and one set of cutlery for each person living in the house. At each meal time each person at table would retrieve his plate, eat the savoury part of the meal on one side of the plate wipe it with bread and then turn the plate over to eat the cheese course or dessert on the other side.

The 'upstairs' was just one large area covering the one room and 'cellier' (wine store) below. It had been used for storing grain and the numerous receptacles partially full of water scattered here and there indicated that the roof was in great need of being replaced. 'Pas de problème' said Madame from the Agence, 'I will find you an artisan, good but cheap'. Well he did prove to be cheap when we received his 'devis' (estimate) a couple of months after we'd bought the house but the vendor's husband and a neighbour both wrote to us 6 months later when we were back in the UK to warn us that the work was being badly done. I rushed back to France, saw the price tags on the new ladder and all of the tools, learned that the 'artisan' had just come out of prison, had never done a roof or any other kind of building work before and that he was Madame's brother looking for a job! Needless to say, a stand had to be made and the neighbour was quite impressed when I sacked the 'cowboy' on the spot with lots of verbal encouragement and threats of violence towards the poor man from the vendor's husband! He and his wife had sold us the house but he still felt responsible for it!

Granny's cottage had exactly the same layout as the room in the main house – open fire, sink with 'oeil du bac' and a ladder outside to the 'grenier' above where grain had been stored but was now full of old bits of pottery crocks and clothing items – including several local ladies' bonnets known as 'kichenotte'. These bonnets which were worn close to the face with sides protruding forwards were tied under the chin with a ribbon and are said to date from the 100 Years War when they were worn by young girls to avoid being kissed by English soldiers – 'Kiss-me-Nots'! Probably not a true story!

We planned to use this cottage as a bedroom for all of us, creating private sleeping quarters as best we could using bookcases, until we could afford to create bedrooms in the main house with the single room in the house being used as a living kitchen.

The two-roomed cottage had one room with the same layout as the other cottage and the room in the main house but the second room had a trapdoor giving access to under the floorboards under which was a shallow square hole in the underlying clay; this was the 'coolbox' where food could be kept reasonably fresh. There was also a narrow staircase leading up to a room with an impossibly low ceiling. Apparently this house had been home and workshop to a dwarf shoemaker for many years. Known as 'Le Capitaine' he was renowned – and disliked – for his practical jokes in the hamlet. He had once, for instance, taken wild duck eggs from a nest by the village pond and placed them in the bed of a sick woman to hatch! When he was alive, the hamlet comprised of at least 22 homes and had its own school.

This cottage, we decided, would be the first thing to get our tender and loving care as it would make a great little 'gîte' and could provide us with some seasonal income once modernised but it really was a complete ruin and had been unoccupied since the Second World War. At that time it had been home to a single woman and her children; Apparently she had left under a cloud for having fraternised with soldiers from the occupying German army!

We noticed that our property didn't have a well while other properties did but there was a communal well on the other side of the road, next to the village pond, together with a very fine bread oven on the front of which was the date of construction – 1808 – the initials IDP (Ita Diis Placuit) (Thus may it please God) and the name of the builder. A wonderful oven, this was now the property of our future lovely neighbours in which and with whom we were to share memorable 'fête du four' events in the future. Unfortunately the water in the well – some 22 metres underground – was not drinkable owing to the level of nitrates it contained, but there was a mains supply to the property and also an electricity supply.

Now it was time to meet the neighbours – or rather for them to meet us as they had been watching our every move ever since our arrival – of course! We had the impression that nothing happened at Le Sauvage in those days so we were viewed with great interest. Our immediate neighbours, close to retirement, had lived in the hamlet all their married life and Lucienne, the wife had been born there. They had some twenty goats which they milked, a few sheep and 26 hectares of fields and woodland. Their three sons were all married and lived elsewhere, not far away, but none were interested in continuing with the farm once their parents retired. They also had an orchard, a small vineyard, a productive 'potager' – and they viewed us with incredulity as to why an English family should want to come 'se cacher dans ce lieu perdu'! In their living kitchen we tasted Paul's 'vin de la vigne' and Lucienne's 'tarte aux prunes' which she eventually admitted had been made with plums they'd picked from our future plum trees! (Well, they'd have gone to waste otherwise!). We found them really honest, genuine and friendly people and they very soon became wonderful friends and neighbours; they have remained so over the years and I think we would do anything for them, and they for us. Another house was lived in by a very elderly couple, Pierre and Thérèse, and their two middle-aged sons. One of them was in work but the other stayed at home to help with the gardening and chores around the house; both were somewhat 'simple-minded', the result of intermarriage. The wife was very quick to come round, having heard that we were thinking of buying in the hamlet. She came with one son pushing a wheelbarrow which was very full of very large ripe tomatoes for us! Once we told her that we were indeed thinking of coming to live in Le Sauvage she burst into tears – of joy! – and immediately insisted on taking Sue on a long walk around the hamlet and into the forest, pointing out houses, remains of houses and explaining who had lived there and what they had done, as well as every tree (especially the chestnut trees), explaining that it was 'intérdit' (forbidden) to pick chestnuts off the ground without their owners' permission until after 'La Toussaint' – All Saints' Day, the 1st of November. If we wanted to collect snails, they had to have an opening of the shell of a certain size or the Gendarmes would arrest you (!) always full of advice which she imposed on us over the years until she died, she was the archetypal village gossip 'corbeau' (crow), busybody and mixture of sweet old lady and interfering dragon...

Her husband was a truly kindly man who had fought

against 'les Boches' and had had a very hard life working as a 'domestique' (farm labourer) on various farms and coping with his trouble-making wife and two slightly mentally handicapped sons. Unfortunately he died a couple of years after we had moved in – in Sue's arms.

While Sue was being shown around by Thérèse I'd bumped into a resident from the next hamlet, just 1km away, accompanied by his hunting dog, he had his shotgun in the crook of his arm. 'Ah, vous êtes l'anglais, vous' (ah, you're the English bloke). 'Oui, Monsieur, et vous, vous êtes de Croutelle et vous êtes en train de vous promener avec votre chien? Bonjour!' (yes I am and you must be from Croutelle, out walking your dog. Hello) 'Ol est bizarre, on vous comprends!' (that's strange, one can understand what you're saying!). Well that's because I'm speaking to you in French! 'Ol est bizarre, y vous comprends!' and off he went, scratching his head. ('Ol' = it; 'Y' = I) The only other house which was lived in had been divided into two following the death of the man of the house. In France, under Napoleonic law, when either the husband or the wife dies, the surviving spouse inherits half of the family home with the other half being divided between the children. The children or the surviving spouse are not allowed to sell or dispose of their share of the property without the consent of all and the spouse is allowed to stay in the house until his or her death unless all agree to sell. In this case the house had been physically divided into two smaller houses and one half was lived in by the surviving wife and her only son, the only daughter having sold her share of the house to 'gens du Nord' and it was used as a holiday home. This mother and son lived in very basic accommodation although the house did have upstairs rooms on two floors which were not used. The original house must have been the largest and richest property in the village in the past – before this seemingly daft law had led to it being divided-up.

The only other large property in the hamlet was inhabited by a dog, an Alsatian called Freda! Her owner had died the previous year and Freda had been left there ever since, attached to a long chain she guarded the house and the ex-proprietor's daughter came every day to feed her; the property consisting of a large house similar to ours and with three other cottages – including one which had been the village school in the past – was up for sale too. Somehow it didn't have the same appeal as the one we were interested in. The other properties which were liveable in were holiday homes and we didn't meet the owners until after we'd moved in. The pair of houses backing onto 'Le Capitaine's cottage' had been the property of Ernest, Aristide's brother, our vendor's father – and because the two brothers had fallen out with each other, Ernest had sold his property to our immediate and 'absent' neighbour through a 'vente rentée' scheme. This is a fascinating arrangement where the acquirer pays a certain lump sum of money, the amount of which is decided on by the notaire and is called 'le bouquet', and who then undertakes to pay an annual rent until the death of the vendor when the property becomes his. Obviously, sometimes the acquirer can die first but in this case he was very 'lucky' as Ernest and his wife had both died – in the same month – within a couple of years of signing the contract. (Both Ernest and his wife had also been born in the same month of the same year!). Another fascinating term which figured on the contract was that the acquirer agreed to look after Ernest 'et de le recevoir à sa table' (feed him at his table) in the event of Ernest's wife dying before him! Unfortunately, the acquirer had done nothing to the property since Ernest's death in the 1960's and it was now in a terrible state of decay.

So, if we moved in here, we would be in a tiny village with seven other people – all older than Sue and I and with no other children for ours to play with. We thought about this and then decided to go to the Mairie in order to find out more about the 'commune'. We knew that the Mayor in France was a very important and quite powerful person. Elected by permanent residents in the 'commune' he or she is the person who conducts marriages, registers births, oversees the village school's activities, is responsible for the church building and who seals your coffin when you die! He proved to be very helpful – and very interested in us, albeit perplexed as to why an English family should want to come and live in such a place as his 'commune'. He knew, but didn't understand why, the one English holiday home in his commune – in Le Sauvage – had a nameplate on the wall on which was written 'The Mousetrap'. He asked what the significance of this was as no one in the commune had a nameplate on their house. People, after all, were simply known by their name and the hamlet where they lived. Often little hamlets were simply called by the name of a resident – 'Chez Bertrand', 'Chez Clion', etc. He was intrigued and enquired if we would be calling our house something. We explained what 'mousetrap' meant but he couldn't understand why anyone should want to call their house after a device for catching mice and when we humorously suggested that as our future home was much bigger we would call it the 'Rat Trap' we were met by a blank stare and the inevitable Gallic shrug of the shoulders which usually means 'ils sont fous ces anglais'! English humour didn't go down well then, and it still doesn't today! 'Do you know the people in the holiday home?' 'No' we said. 'Mais ce sont des anglais!' How many times in future years were we asked if we knew the latest British arrivals! Apparently, all English people abroad know each other!!

By now, we had such a warm feeling about Le Sauvage, the house, the neighbours and the wonderfully unspoiled countryside that the very next day we returned to see Mme l'agente immobilière and promised to buy. Once given, our word would be binding and we returned to County Durham full of excitement.

3

A Banquet?

Over the next 10 months, we set about selling our house in the UK, moved into rented accommodation, accepted Madame's offer of finding a 'reliable artisan who would work quickly and well' to re-roof the house in Le Sauvage, signed contracts and paid-up, sacked the artisan and found others to finish the work and install a septic tank and a basic bathroom and then contacted the French 'Douane' service. This was to give us our first taste of what was to become 27 years of difficult relations with the French Administrative system! No problem with furniture or with the cat and the dog – just a visit to the vet 24 hours before sailing to receive a certificate of health was all that was necessary – but a couple of hamsters?! Telephone calls to the Consular Services in London resulted in silence when hamsters were mentioned. 'May we take my daughter's hamsters to France?' 'We do not know.' 'Shall I just put them in my pocket and say nothing when we land in France?' 'We have no advice to give you, Monsieur'. It was important to Natalie that her hamsters accompany us and so we rigged-up a system of getting water and food into the cage which was placed out of sight at the back of the motor caravan and headed off to Portsmouth to catch the ferry in July.

As instructed, we reported to 'Animal Health' at the port and the paperwork for cat and Border Collie were all in order; 'Good luck', said the Custom's Officer. 'Why do we need luck?' 'Well, your papers are in order but let's just say it would be best to keep the dog's head down when you land in France!' 'But if they won't let the dog in, what can we do?' 'Well you can't bring her back Sir...' Chilling thoughts came to us of our poor Mollie spending the rest of her life on the sea between France and the UK! We joined the queue of vehicles for the ferry and the next thing we knew was a different Custom's Officer tapping on the car window. 'Excuse me Sir, I have reason to believe that you have a dog in your vehicle'. 'Yes, we have; and a cat.' 'Well you do realise that you can't bring them back into the country when you return to the UK after your holiday Sir?' 'Yes, of course, they're emigrating; we've been through 'Animal Health' and all is in order.' 'Oh I am sorry Sir, it's just that there was a rather zealous fellow passenger who thought that we should know he'd spotted the dog in your vehicle ...' Brittany Ferries were excellent and allowed us as much access to the vehicle as we wanted during the overnight crossing – and we did indeed keep the dog's head down as we drove into Caen. When we arrived at Le Sauvage later that day we really did feel as though we were 'coming home'; it just seemed natural to us and even Mollie the Border Collie and the cat seemed happy. The hamsters too had survived the journey and were put into their quarters in one of the outbuildings. Then, tragedy! The hamsters were later found to be missing and we found evidence of a visit having been made by Le Sauvage 'mulots' (small rats)! After all that fuss and the care we'd taken to get them safely to France!

A rabbit was given by our kind neighbours in compensation but we didn't dare say to the children that the rabbit was one that had been destined for the table. All of our neighbours kept and bred rabbits for this very purpose – as we were also soon to do... We 'moved-in' and spent a wonderful Summer just cleaning and clearing rubbish – inside and outside. The only problem was that over the 6 weeks we were there, we had 72 visitors from the UK! Some were friends, some were people who said they knew us or of us and we couldn't remember them! Some wanted to stay –'but we have no bedrooms!' – Some wanted to camp and 'make themselves "useful"' while others were just curious and needed entertaining. Most arrived unannounced and we realised that what we were doing in moving here was also what others were thinking of doing – but had never got round to.

The most memorable event of that Summer, however, was a banquet which will forever remain in our memory, prepared for us by the vendor's wife. She had turned-up very early one morning with her husband lurching into the yard in their battered Citroën 'Ami' Estate car which was brim full of blackened pots and pans, jars of preserves, boxes of bottles and vegetables. 'J'ai tout le nécessaire' she smilingly declared giving us all three large, very noisy, limpet-like kisses. Her husband gave me a firm handshake, pecked the three children and gave Sue three lingering kisses and with a broad smile said 'for your lovely eyes I have brought you a present for your garden'. This was a wonderful, old wooden wheelbarrow and obviously Sue was delighted. They then took-over our one and only room where Madame had spent her youth and set-to immediately with the job in hand; she was going to give us 'un repas de chez-nous', indicating that we would be eating solely home-produced food served in the local way. We started taking mental notes – all this would be useful if we were really to become paysans! The first job, after Monsieur had lit a fire in the large open hearth, was to hang a cauldron of soup over the flames by means of the 'cremaillère'. Next to the fire were placed two large, oval, black 'faitouts' or stew pots so their contents could be warmed and the table was then set. One bowl-shaped plate per person, a tumbler, a large soup spoon, a knife and fork and a small tea towel sized serviette! We were seven in all – 5 of us and two of them – but places were set for 9. 'Your good neighbours are coming for the dessert', we were informed, 'at 4 o'clock'. Sue and I looked at each other – it was only 11.45 and we were about to start eating!

First of all we had the 'apéritif' to whet the appetite and this was our first taste of pineau – a drink made by Monsieur from the grapes grown on the front of the house. We asked, of course how it was made and were very surprised to hear how simple it was. The ripe grapes are picked, crushed and the juice immediately filtered before it has time to ferment. Eau de vie (cognac) is then added to the juice with a dosage of about two thirds juice to one third cognac until the final alcohol content is about 17°. You then wait a few weeks before tasting. A deposit will have formed so the mixture is then decanted or filtered. When served chilled it is really delicious;

naturally sweet, nothing at all is added. This was accompanied by walnuts from the tree in the yard. Some were 'nature' whilst others had been soaked in either strong brine or a sugar solution and then allowed to dry – somewhat healthier than artificially-flavoured crisps.

The 'potage' or soup was then transferred from the fire to the table and a ladle-full was scooped into each plate. A bit thin and rather bland this, and a bit disappointing. It had apparently been made from a marrow bone, a leek and a potato. The best part was the 'godaille' which is a locally traditional way to finish the soup. Whether this word originates from the English 'good ale', dating back to the 100 Years' War or not is irrelevant but it consists of pouring some red wine into the nearly empty soup dish and swilling the greasy remains around before offering it up directly to your mouth. Bread, which is not eaten with the soup, is then used to wipe the plate dry! We did notice looks of incomprehension when we tilted our plates away from us in order to finish the last drops. They, of course, were tilting their plates towards themselves...

Then followed radishes from the garden, prepared with their root cut-off but with a couple of centimetres of leaves left on. The way to eat them was to hold the radish by its leaves and then to dip it in salt, adding a small piece of butter – if you could get it to stick. Bread accompanied the radishes, but not bread and butter. While it might have been easier to put the butter on the bread rather than on the radish, this was not done. One never butters bread in this part of France but butter is served with salami or 'saucisson sec', salted ham, melon or radishes – and bread is an accompaniment. A boiled egg and sliced tomato salad followed, with chopped parsley, chopped chives and home-brewed vinaigrette (soured wine!); an acquired taste... Then followed a very grand course – a 'Farci Poitevin' – a dish found no where else consisting of masses of finely cut (with scissors usually) spinach, lettuce, parsley, garlic, onion and chard to which is added a dozen or more eggs and cubes of fatty, salted pork. The mixture is then boiled for a consider-able time, enveloped in cabbage leaves, a tea towel and placed in a net. The green, domed 'pudding' is presented with great pomp and can be eaten warm as it comes out of the cauldron or later cold or, in our case, cut into 2cm thick slices and fried. This majestic dish is a matter of pride for ladies in the area and we have since been to several village evening meals where several farcis have appeared with their cooks carefully eyeing their neigh-bours' efforts with a critical and jealous eye! I suppose it's this area of France's answer to 'bubble and squeak'. (See in the cooking chapter for the recipe).

Already full, we were allowed to rest and recover somewhat while the children were allowed to run around outside. After a few minutes they returned with a worried look on their faces and a somewhat apprehensive Justin. Natalie whispered that they'd played around the village well and that when Justin had tried to turn the handle which held the rope, he'd lost control of it and the rope had shot down to the bottom – 22 metres below. Monsieur had already talked about the well when, in the past, it had been the only source of water for the house and it had been his job every morning to fetch water from the well for the cows before milking. I felt worried that if we mentioned Justin's 'problem' to him Justin could come across as an undisciplined child and poor Justin would feel embarrassed, so nothing was said.

Now for the plat de résistance: home-reared roast chicken and green beans freshly picked. Two whole chickens, complete with feet and heads appeared from the tureens by the fire. They had been cooked 'nature' with just garlic and herbs – and delicious they did smell! But Natalie started crying at the sight of the heads and made it quite clear she wouldn't be eating any...Fearful of creating a 'diplomatic' incident, I hissed 'you will eat it, you like chicken and you know where chickens come from; we've reared enough over the years'. 'Yes, but they've got their heads on; it's like eating a pet – you wouldn't eat Molly if she was served-up!'. « Ca ne fait rien si elle n'aime pas le poulet, il y a du lapin si elle préfère.»

An inward Argghh!, the thought of trying to get Natalie to eat one of the brothers or sisters of her rabbit which were still in the concrete cage outside would be met with even more resistance! 'Non, non Madame, pas de problème, elle aime bien le poulet, merci'... The beans had been tossed in butter and chopped shallots after having been boiled. No potatoes, but lots of bread again – that essential accessory for wiping the plate clean again between courses!

Then the cheese course. For conversation, we mentioned that in the UK we ate dessert before the cheese course but this was met with that Gallic look of complete incomprehension; and if you think about it, it is logical to stay with savoury dishes and to finish with sweet dishes! There was no cheese 'board' and the choice was between goat's cheese and goat's cheese! They had been made in the next village and one was a fresh, soft variety containing chopped chives and chervil, the second, an older, drier variety which was more strongly flavoured. Both were delicious with yet more bread and more wine. We'd been given water and wine all through the meal – not different wines specially chosen for each course, just rough, deep red wine from Monsieur's vines; again, an acquired taste but it did seem to improve with each successive glassful! The children were offered wine diluted with water, which is usual in the area. At some point Justin had whispered to me 'why does Monsieur always serve himself from a different bottle, kept under the table?' Monsieur didn't understand English, but he'd noticed the whispering and he had quickly guessed what had been said. We would have to get used to being observed closely. We were different, even exotic to these people; we were 'étrangers' – strange-ers and our every move would be scrutinised for a long time. 'Tell the "petit bonhomme" that I am drinking my "piquette" which isn't good enough to serve to guests'. His 'piquette' was in fact the result of pouring water onto the lees or sediment of the wine once it had been decanted off; another example of the 'waste not, want not' philosophy of these country folk. Surprisingly, or not! The time was now approaching 4pm and our dear nearest neighbours appeared, as announced, bearing 'un gateau sec' to go with the bottled peaches, plums, cherries, etc (from the garden of course) which had been steeped in spirits over some months. This was called the 'confiture de vieux garçon' (old bachelor's preserve!). The alcohol had been made from the plums from the trees in the yard and the gateau sec turned out to be a sort of shortbread.

While coffee was being prepared Paul, the neighbour had winked at me and indicated that I should slip outside with him. Once in front of the house, he pointed to the 20 metres of coiled rope which he'd managed to fish out of the well! Obviously, the children had been seen playing and the scene had not gone unnoticed! Paul put his finger to his lips and I felt a certain complicity with him, and thanked him for his discretion...

Coffee and 'goute' ended this banquet, goute (a drop) being a strong, home-made liquor. This one was 'Poire William'; delicious! This was when we made the 'faux pas' by offering Madame the large box of After Eight chocolates we'd brought. We never had one! (each chocolate represented a stone in the wall of her house – her 'heritage' (inheritance) which she'd sold to us...)

We'd sat down on those low, hard, straw-covered, kitchen chairs at 12 noon and we eventually got up from the table, feeling very replete, strangely tired and with a muzzy head nearly six hours later. But the time had flown. During the long gaps between the different courses we'd been able to ask so many questions concerning where we would now be living for the foreseeable future and, of course we were grilled (again) about why we had wanted to come, what we were going to do, what we thought about France, Europe, les 'Boches', English weather, Margaret Thatcher, etc, etc...truly a wonderful experience. That night, when Sue wrote in her diary the day's events, she just wrote 'today we had lunch'!!

4

The Slate and the Serviette

When the end of August came I headed back to the UK with the two older children while Sue was left with the task of seeing if the plan could work – that of living day to day in France outside the holiday period with a child at school. If these weeks between 'la rentrée' and the 'Toussaint' holiday could be deemed a success; I would resign from my job and come across in November with another child during which time child Number 3 went off on a school exchange to France! Then, at Christmas 1989, I would move across with the last child.

The plan actually worked wonderfully... Sue reckons the period between September and Christmas of that year was one of the happiest of her life. Armed with a credit card and a bike she camped in the house, sleeping on a camp bed and cooking on a wood burning stove which we'd bought for 500 francs (£50) as a result of spotting a small ad in one of the baker's vans which called in at Le Sauvage five days a week.

Here are her impressions of that idyllic time:

During that month of August 1989, plans had gone ahead for preparing Richard, our youngest child, for school. He had been enrolled in the local Primary school which was in fact known as a 'regroupement péda-gogique' whereby two small schools in two separate villages (communes) whose numbers had dropped to such an extent that they were considered as being one school on two sites. The mayor had informed us that Richard would be attending the 'maternelle' section of the school which was furthest from Le Sauvage in the next commune, some 7kms away.

To our surprise, Richard's future teacher contacted us and kindly invited us to her house for afternoon cakes and drinks and to meet her two boys who also attended the school. It proved to be a very pleasant occasion for the grown-ups but shyness overcame Richard and the whole experience only served to emphasise the sheer difference between French and English ways of family life; what struck us was the way all French children are encouraged to greet everyone in the room, one by one, with one sideways kiss and a 'bonjour', with the same process when people leave, replacing the bonjour with 'au revoir'!

It was during this afternoon 'goûter' that we learned of the terrible thing which had happened to another boy of Richard's age, and who would be in the same class, who had caught his hand in the conveyor feed belt at his parents' goat farm and had lost several fingers. Learning of this traumatised Richard but he was later to be amazed and impressed to see how his new friend coped with everyday life in spite of this terrible handicap.

On one day in that August, as a family, we all took to our push-bikes and rode along the country lanes to find Richard's new school. It was quite an adventure for Richard as he hadn't been riding a bike for long but when we arrived he was happy to see the front of his new school, puffed-out though he was.

Once Garry and the other two children had left, the first day of the new school year quickly arrived. The mayor had been to see us again and had explained how Richard would be able to catch the school minibus every morning which stopped at the lane end round the corner, and be brought home again in the evening, giving us the approximate times for Mum and child to wait. The school bag was packed with all the requested items we had to supply – notably a slate on which each child had to write whatever answer the teacher asked and a stick of chalk, pencils, crayons, a ruler and a note book duly went into the bag and we hoped we'd followed all of the instructions correctly. Only later were we told that we'd forgotten a most important item – a cloth serviette with Richard's name on it for tying around his neck at lunch time!

It was a lovely sunny morning and as we walked along to the 'bus stop' we saw a group of beautiful roe deer in a field. They heard us and headed off with their white rumps bobbing up and down into the distance. Here was the place where the mayor had told us to stand for the bus and here we waited with me chattering away to keep Richard distracted as he was looking decidedly nervous!

Ten minutes later we were still waiting when a car drew up alongside us. A kindly-looking man asked us something I didn't entirely understand; he kept saying 'car' ('le car scolaire' means the school bus!) but we were waiting for a minibus! He indicated on his watch that we'd missed it and he offered to take Richard in his car to catch it up. I let Richard climb in next to the man...and drive off into the unknown...and then I realised what I'd done and fretted all the way back home, fighting back the tears as I struggled with the irresponsible way I'd abandoned my child to a stranger! I poured my heart out in my pigeon French to Lucienne in her farmyard whilst waiting for the baker's van to arrive on his rounds and she comforted me saying that she thought she knew who the strange man must have been; not to worry, he had children at the same school and during the afternoon I had a visit from the mother of the child who'd lost his fingers in that terrible accident and she assured me that she'd seen Richard getting off 'le car' and go into school, albeit very reluctantly...

OUF! (phew), as the French say! So that was that, Richard's first day at school.

There are, however, two sequels to the story:

The first is that what we hadn't realised when we'd been to see the school on our bikes was that there are two entrances; we'd shown Richard the one which led onto the playground and the school bus had stopped at a second one, round the other side, and as he didn't recognise it he refused to get off the bus! He thought he'd been taken to the wrong school and apparently had cried and clung to his seat until coaxed off the bus...

The second is that we'd given him a box of chocolates to offer to his new school friends on that first day. He'd given them to his teacher in the morning who'd kept them safely on her desk next to the French-English dictionary which with foresight she'd provided in case of problems with her first foreign student! At the end of the school day the whole class was lined-up in single file facing Richard who was handed his box of chocolates. Each child took one and...thanked him with a kiss! 'Don't you ever give me a box of chocolates to share again Mum' he expostulated, wiping his face, when he got home! He also came home with a note from the teacher indicating that 'les puces sont arrivées' (head lice had been detected at the school) and all should go to the pharmacy to buy the necessary product to combat the infection; also on the note was the parental rota for the providing of potatoes for the school canteen! The sooner we got a vegetable garden planted the better!

Richard was very thoughtful and tired during that first evening. I had explained to him that he would probably understand very little of what was being said during the day but advised him to smile a lot, be polite and if asked 'comment tu t'appelles' to simply answer 'Richard'. I later learned that he'd spent the day saying 'Richard' a lot! Apparently everyone, staff and children, had been very kind to him and he was treated as a bit of a celebrity with many children wanting 'le petit anglais' to be their friend.

His teacher being aware that Richard spoke no French and was new to the French system put him in a class lower than his age group (CP) so that he might cope with schooling more easily. No pressure was put onto him and it was thanks to his keenness and interest to learn that he was accepted and did succeed very quickly. He was a happy child from day one except on one occasion when I was told he was seen crying at the dinner table; apparently the dinner lady had tried to force him to eat spinach which he hated – and still hates! CP (Cours Préparatoire) is the top class in the Infant ('Maternelle') section in French Primary Education; the organisation is as follows: Petite Section (age 4), Moyenne Section, Grande Section, Cours Préparatoire. Then follows Cours Elémentaire 1 and 2, and finishing with Cours Moyen 1 and 2 before all go on into Secondary education at a 'Collège' at the age of 11.

French children, from a very early age, are given homework to do every evening for the next day. This was fascinating for me for I was learning alongside my 7-year old son the rudiments of grammar and even sometimes a simple poem or song which had to be learned by heart. I tried to insist that homework was done as soon as Richard arrived home so that he could relax and have fun afterwards but he quickly made the point that he knew his comrades went home to 'quatre-heures' ('four o'clocks') which is a French ritual, heavily endorsed by indulgent French mothers, by which their children's tummies are filled with energy-giving snacks as soon as they get home. This goûter is usually hunks of bread or 'brioche' covered with a thick layer of chocolate spread accompanied by chocolate-flavoured milk. I conceded but Richard, still having English taste buds, preferred Marmite sandwiches!

After homework was done he would go outside and often play with Mollie the Border Collie. After a few weeks of school I heard him playing football in the garden and shouting instructions to the dog in French. I was dumb-struck; I thought 'he's made it!' On some warm Autumn evenings, we would go for a walk in our local woods. It was a great opportunity for exploration. There were always new little creatures to discover – bright emerald-green salamanders, slithering grass snakes and red squirrels; and on some rainy days, bright orange slugs littering our path. We would gather sticks in a large chestnut basket – the French equivalent of a trug which we'd inherited in the house – sticks to light the evening fire when the nights started drawing-in. We looked out for various animal tracks and signs and loved looking them up in the Collins guide when we got home. We both had a bike so sometimes I would save the local shopping to do in the local town of Sauzé-Vaussais 5kms away for Richard's return from school and we would pedal with a cardboard box strapped onto the backs of our bikes to carry the shopping home in. My sense of orientation isn't too good and Richard was amazed at how many different routes we could take in order to get home after our shopping trips. The truth being, many of the country lanes looked alike to me and there was a distinct lack of road signs back to Le Sauvage! As time went on, Richard's sense of direction proved to be better than mine and he would guide us back home and quite rightly, he chose routes with less uphill stretches! As he gained confidence at school and he was rewarded for his French reading abilities (he had already learned to read in English before we'd left the UK) by being promoted from CP to CE1 – the right year for his age. With growing confidence at school, he also became the 'man about the house' once back home in the evening. He would busy himself with useful projects designed to make our daily life easier – chopping sticks for the fire, banging long nails into bits of wood to make a coat hanger and helping to convert pallets into compost bins. A job he liked very much was feeding the chickens with corn and kitchen scraps and collecting the beautiful brown eggs and, later in the evening, locking the hen-house door against Mr Fox's night-time visits. Perhaps his very favourite job was digging into the compost bins to find knots of worms to give the hens a special treat. We dug over a small plot of a field and made our very first vegetable garden, proudly planting lettuce, radishes and a few late potatoes in the hope that the warm Autumn sun would favour their harvest. However, the end of Autumn became very wet with the farmyard turning into a quagmire and those bright orange slugs got to the lettuces and radishes before we could! Never mind, we wouldn't go hungry for one morning at the school bus stop (where we'd been too late on the first morning but never late after that!) one of the other Mums who was waiting with her children proudly presented me with a huge carrier bag of mushrooms she'd picked. What a treat! I wasn't actually familiar with the variety but was assured that they were very delicious if fried with butter, garlic and parsley. That evening, Richard prepared slices of toast and I set-to to cook the 'souchettes' as they were called. They did indeed smell delicious as they were gently frying on the wood burner and we thoroughly enjoyed a large plateful each. Twenty minutes later, Richard looked deathly white and complained of a tummy ache. I didn't have the time to sympathise with him before I too felt decidedly peaky. We both spent the evening and night rushing in and out of our makeshift bathroom and we slept-in on the following morning. Fortunately there was no school on that day. As it was a Saturday and one of the days the baker called, our neighbour came round to see why I'd missed buying bread and discovered us both still looking rather seedy.

Word soon got around about our mushroom poisoning experience and even the Mayor honoured us with a special visit and he seemed to feel almost responsible for the mishap! I felt sorry for us but also sorry for the poor woman who'd given us the 'souchettes' in good faith – although they had turned out to be a poisoned gift! Our neighbour elucidated us as to what I had done wrong; we weren't supposed to eat the stalks – only the caps! 'Il faut les déguster sans les pieds!' The event caused considerable hilarity in the commune but gathering and eating wild mushrooms found in the forest is a popular – if potentially dangerous activity! It's also a game of 'hide and seek' as many people take it very seriously and know exactly where and when to find certain varieties and, of course, this is all a great secret; a 'chasseur de champignons' will never divulge his secrets and will go to considerable lengths to put other interested parties off the scent! Every year, many people do actually die from mushroom poisoning in France as a result of mistakenly picking the wrong variety. If in doubt about a specimen, one is supposed to go to any local chemist shop and receive expert, free advice from the shop assistants who have all been trained in mushroom identification! Poor Richard came in for 'a bit of stick' at school and for years wouldn't touch any mushrooms. Later, he became an expert 'chasseur de champignons' himself – but he too won't divulge his secret places!

So during this time that Richard was 'blossoming' as a

new little French boy and comforting us that our family project was working well so far, Sue was also improving her communication skills in French at an impressive rate. My mother had been a Walloon Belgian and so I had a certain facility in French but Sue had just 'O level French GCE' under her belt when she'd arrived at Le Sauvage so she had 'beaucoup de pain sur la planche' and would have to furnish considerable efforts if she were to integrate into the French community. Short daily conversations at the bus stop and at the baker's van, followed by cups of coffee 'chez la voisine' were a great help – as was Richard's homework! She therefore found herself in a complete 'bain linguistique' with no other English-speakers around to fall back on and this, we still feel today, was the very best way to improve her skills. So quick was her progress that just three months later she would be employed as a language assistant in a local secondary school and giving English lessons at Evening Classes for adults in three local towns! But for now, in October, with Richard settled we could enjoy a family half-term holiday together – except for Justin, the older son who at the age of 12 had been sent on a school exchange to another part of France, to improve his French skills away from the family! At the end of the week it was our daughter Natalie's turn to try and cope with a new life in our newly adopted country. We always knew that this part of the project would be most difficult to succeed. Taking an adolescent girl away from her friends was always going to be problematic and whilst she could communicate a bit in French after 3 years of lessons in the comprehensive school in Durham, getting up at 6.30am to catch a school bus which would take her to the secondary school 20kms away for lessons which lasted from 8.00am until 5.00pm and where the school regime was light years away from that in the UK was going to prove to be exhausting and potentially very frightening for her. We had chosen this 'college' rather than a more local one as it was reputed to have a 'section bilingue' where some of the lessons were supposedly given in English; this proved to be not exactly the case... Monsieur le Principal was very keen indeed to have 'une vraie anglaise' as a pupil in his 'Section Bilingue' of which he was very proud and Madame le Principal Adjointe took her under her wing from the start. This was not the case, however, for her English teacher who must have felt a bit threatened to have an English-speaker in his lessons as from the start his favourite tack was to quiz Natalie on points of English grammar. As Natalie, like all British children at that time, had never done any grammar at all (beyond knowing that a 'verb' was a 'doing' word and a noun was what things were) he quickly realised this fact and used it regularly as his way of empowering himself by demonstrating to the whole class that he knew all about English grammar whereas l'anglaise didn't. What a tragic start to a new school career! This was further compounded as one of Natalie's favourite activities at school in Durham had been creative writing, and there was nothing creative about English lessons in France...another favourite creative activity had been drama lessons, and that didn't exist in France either. School plays were prepared – but this was 'theatre', not drama; no self-expression, and her third favourite activity had been playing the flute in the school orchestra...The only way to get to play the flute at this school was to give up free time on Wednesday afternoons, when there was no school, and to attend 'solfège' lessons; this was music theory, the grammar of music, divorced from playing an instrument...and there was no school orchestra, or any other musical group. No out-of-school clubs at all! All in all, the first term was a catastrophe for poor Natalie and Sue was summoned to the Collège to face the 'Conseil de Classe' to account for Natalie's lack of progress. The Conseil is actually a great thing which didn't exist in the UK in those days. All of the teachers of the class get together with elected parent and pupil representatives and, chaired by the Head or Deputy, each child's performance in each subject is discussed at the end of each term. Individual parents do not usually attend but a special dispensation was made for Natalie's case. Sue did her very best to defend Natalie and to try and get the different teachers to feel some empathy for an adolescent girl who'd been plunged into an environment which was totally 'foreign' to her. Sue, too, found this new experience of facing a 'board' of mostly critical 'fonctionaires' (teachers are civil servants in France) somewhat threatening...Ah, French administration! How much we were to fight against it over the ensuing years! Clearly, having a child from 'elsewhere' with different experiences and used to doing things differently was a bit of a challenge for some of these educators who were used to giving 'magisterial' lessons in which they were master of their subject and minions were supposed to listen in silence, grateful for the pearls of wisdom which were thrown in their direction! But, to be fair, some teachers were, in private, quite supportive. The maths teacher thought that Natalie had an enquiring mind, which he liked and he was also the school representative for health insurance for teachers and was concerned that our family should be properly covered. 'It's not like in England; health cover is not totally free in France; you must get 'top-up' cover when your husband comes'. The Deputy Head thought that Monsieur might like to work at the college if he wanted a job when he came... I had returned to Durham after the Autumn half term break not too happy about Nats and met up again with Justin, fresh from his stay with a French family in Montdidier. He hadn't had a wonderful time either and was in no way looking forward to moving to France full-time! Here was good news when I was due to hand-in my resignation the next day! A supportive father-son conversation ensued. Apparently Justin's correspondent's father was a keen hunter (anyone can basically hunt on anyone's land in France if they pass a test) and he had been invited to join a full-scale deer hunt which had become a bit too much for Justin. He'd witnessed a deer being shot and then its throat cut before being skinned and gutted and when Justin had turned pale his correspondent friend had made a bit of fun of him. It's true that whenever the local butcher in Cumbria had come round to us on a weekend to slaughter our pigs or sheep at home, he'd always gone off with a friend – as did the other children and even Mollie had taken to lying under the butcher's car and growling if he approached her! There was also one occasion when the butcher had inflated a pig's bladder, tied a knot in it and thrown it in Justin's direction saying 'here's a football for ya' this had not made Justin want to become a butcher or to want to have anything to do with the process. He didn't mind eating home-made Cumberland sausage or home-reared turkey at Christmas, however! Another reason for wanting to stay in the UK was that his best friend had a 3-wheeler motorbike and very often the two of them would drive it over his friend's father's fields. Fortunately, I was able to – truthfully – say that he'd have his own 'mobylette' (moped) in 18 months time as this is what most French children had for their 14th birthday but in the UK he would have to wait until he was 16. That clinched the deal – especially when he realised that he could apply his Technic Lego skills onto dismantling mopeds as a hobby! In fact, once in France, he was able to pursue this 'dream' and became determined to spend the rest of his life as a mobylette and 'Solex' mechanic. (Solexes were still quite popular in rural France at that time but I'd only ever seen them before then in old French films, usually ridden by a priest with cassock flowing in the wind – or by gaggles of nuns. Resembling, more or less, a heavy push-bike, they had a 2-stroke engine perched over the front wheel which could be lowered onto the rotating front tyre once you had started pedalling. The engine, kicked into starting by the action of the wheel on the stone cog which gripped the tyre, would then take-over from the pedalling. Affectionately known as 'casse-gueule' [face-smasher] they could indeed be dangerous as if they didn't fire into action immediately, you could be thrown over the handlebars!). (It eventually took Sue and I considerable effort to persuade Justin into having a more ambitious dream and after technical studies he became a trouble-shooting technical expert for VW!)

The next day, Monday 13th November 1989, I handed-in my resignation and then followed two months of preparing for the final move: finding a removal firm (or should I self-drive a truck with a friend), selling our motor-caravan, deciding what to do with 30 or so 13amp electric plugs (!) which would be useless in France, etc. One idea was to offer one as a present to each member of staff on the last day of term; and that's what I did, to the amusement of all. It's surprising how much pleasure you can give to someone by giving them a plug – especially when there's a TV or a coffee-maker attached!

The last school day proved to be very memorable for me indeed as from about 6.50am every 10 or 15 minutes or so, the phone rang with different members of staff at the other end of the line; all were crying off school that day because of sickness and diarrhoea! I immediately thought that the school Christmas dinner which we'd had the previous day must have poisoned everyone and as it was one of my roles as Deputy Head to organise the replacement of absent teachers every day I had to set to and plan to cover absent teachers' lessons. By the time I got to school there were to be some 15 teachers away and I'd used every available teachers' free periods and had the Head in the gym with three classes and myself in the assembly hall with two more. However, when I got to the staff room to pin-up the day's cover timetable all of the colleagues who had phoned-in absent were there sitting and grinning at me! During the final staff meeting at the end of the school day where all received a token present from me, I received a Gold Star Award from the Head for 'Crisis Management' – an honour which I cherish to this day! The removal van came, I handed the motor caravan to its new owner, Justin and I camped in the house over-night and the next day we flew to Paris using up all of the 'Airmiles' I'd managed to accumulate buying things I thought we might miss or not find in rural France – from 'Lakeland Sweaters' to school English history books! Then a 4-hour train trip from Paris to Ruffec in the Charente Département (today it takes 2hours 20mins!) where Sue met us in her 'new' 6-volt Citroën Dyane car. She'd paid 1,000 francs for it and it meant that she could take Natalie to the school bus stop 5 kms away on dark, foggy mornings (but 6 volts doesn't give much headlight power and if you put the windscreen washers on at the same time, the headlights go down to a dull glow which is reflected back from the fog! – Frightening!)

A re-united family again, at last – in something not much better than a hovel; but a clean and comfortable one, with a log fire and a Christmas tree. Richard played the cassette I'd bought him – Cliff Richard singing 'Daddy's Home'! and we had a lovely, simple, family time.

That Christmas period, though, was a bitter-sweet one. I'd managed to bring the flu across from the UK and I was bad-tempered as a result, but perhaps the real problem was that realisation was settling-in as to what I'd actually done – given up a well-paid, responsible and potentially rewarding career with some standing in British society in exchange for unemployed teacher status with little savings to be able to 'do-up' a semi-derelict house in a 'trou perdu' in 'la France profonde' in order to become... « un paysan »!

But this was no time to be maudlin. The furniture van arrived on the 29th December and the entire village turned-out to give a helping hand! We still have lovely mental images of the elderly couple insisting on carrying quite heavy boxes of books, saying 'c'est normal; c'est bien la moindre des choses entre voisins...' (it's the least thing neighbours can do for each other). The light sprinkling of snow on the ground didn't seem to perturb them. Snow?! Nobody had told us that it snowed in this part of France! We'd only been told about the sunshine – that this part of France had the most sunshine after Provence...And, it was cold; very cold! 'Oh, wait a bit, it'll get colder; it got to minus 10° last winter!' This was unexpected! We offered mulled wine for their efforts but that didn't go down too well as they didn't know of it and that shrug and look of incomprehension accompanied a polite refusal! The mince pies were 'intéressant, différent' and, finally 'pas mal' – with 'un coup de rouge' followed by coffee and 'goute' in the still warm coffee cup.

It was then time to get Justin ready for 'collège' and I had to find a job. The children were interested to learn when our plans for improving the house would materialise into having more home comforts. 'When will I get my own bedroom' asked Natalie 'instead of sharing with everyone else'? It was true that all of us sleeping in the same downstairs room of the cottage did seem a bit primitive, even though everyone had their own corner created by tall bookcases... 'Oh, everything in good time' I replied 'let's say 5 or 10 years'. Tears from Natalie 'but I'll be 24 then!' How right she was! 'Right, well I'll sort out a job and go to the bank!' Easy said but that's what I'd have to do...

5

The « Kleenex Teacher »

I had already been to the nearest 'Inspéction Académique' in our County town to ask about a teaching job during the previous October half-term break. Education in France is administered by 'Rectorats' – Regional administrative education offices with an 'Académie' in each constituent County (Département). The Poitou-Charentes Region, is made up of four 'départements', the Vienne, the Charente, the Charente-Maritime and the Deux-Sèvres. The Rectorat employs the teachers and organises Secondary education while the Académies administer Primary education.

I had been well received by Madame l'Inspecteur

d'Académie and whilst she was welcoming and supportive she had made it quite clear that teachers in State
education in France were employed as civil servants
(fonctionnaires) and as such needed to have French
nationality. In addition, a degree issued by a French
university was also required to be able to apply to sit the
qualifying competitive exam (known as the Capès). As
the exam was competitive, only a certain number could
be successful – but I could become a supply teacher...
'Great!' I thought, as I'd been in charge of employing
supply teachers in Durham and knew they were quite
well paid, and it would be a way to getting to know the
French system by working in different establishments!

And so I returned to see Madame l'Inspécteur who
led me through the paperwork required by the Rectorat
in order that my application could be received. She also
warned me that supply teachers (Maitres Auxilaires)
had a low status (they had probably failed the Capès or
hadn't tried to sit the exam!), led a precarious existence
(they could be sent – yes, sent with no choice as to where
they would be working – to any school in the whole of
the Region and for indefinite periods!) and they were
poorly paid ...I later learned that they were known as the
'Kleenex' of the Education National!...so much for my
ambitions of being taken on as an experienced teacher!

Madame made it quite clear that my 20 years of

experience counted in no way as what counted was 'service' (to France!) and not experience; in addition the TEFL I had taken the time to prepare in the UK was of no use in the French educational system. There was a National Curriculum and it had to be adhered-to. Obviously, judging by the amount of time Madame was willing to grant me, and the efforts she made to telephone different services at the Rectorat, I was a rare bird; never before had an Englishman wanted to teach in a school in her region! She strongly suggested that I should eventually try for the Capès, and if successful, obtain 'titularisation' (incumbency of a post), climb up the promotion ladder and enjoy a long career. 'When Europe becomes One in 1992, France will have to accept teachers from other Member countries – be a Maitre-Auxiliare until then'.

There are two Capès exams – 'external' and 'internal'. 'External' means that you can sit the exam as soon as you can show you have a degree from a French university or obtain its equivalent by having your qualifications accepted by a university panel; alternatively, without a degree, you may still sit the exam if you are a mother of three children or are acknowledged as being a highly-qualified sports-person! If you are successful at the 'Capès externe', you will then be sent to any part of France where a teacher of your subject is required as a probationary teacher for one year. This usually means being sent far away from where you live and to a 'difficult' area where no teacher wants to go – an inner city or a 'banlieu'. You may only sit the 'Capès interne' if you have a degree (or be a mother of three children or be a sports-person) and have three years teaching experience as an MA; if successful, you will then be sent to a school within your home region.

So, decisions were made; I would do three years as an MA, get my degree recognised and we would seek French nationality so that I could sit the Capès and become a 'fonctionnaire'. We were keen to be naturalised as it showed commitment to our new country of adoption and we wanted to become more European!

If I chose to become a music teacher MA I wouldn't get a job! Music was little taught in France and the way of teaching it was light years away from the way it was taught in the UK so teaching English was the only possibility for me – and that seemed to be an exciting one to me! A few days after Christmas, Justin joined Natalie at the same college as Natalie while Sue and I remained within earshot of the telephone, hoping that an English teacher would be needed somewhere soon! The phone did go, and it was for the offer of a job! And it was to be at the same college where the two older children were! Great! but it was only for a few hours a week as a language assistant – a job really destined for a language student in the final year of studying for a French degree in a UK university. The student hadn't turned-up and the offer was there. No good for me, but perfect – for Sue! So off she went the very next day, helping French children to improve their English and helping our two to integrate for the rest of the school year – as well as building-up a circle of colleagues and eventually friends, interested – and curious – about our project. The phone went again the next day, and this time it was my turn; a Maitre Aux-iliaire was required for one week for a collège 120 kms away! We had the weekend to find a second car and to find accommodation for me for four nights!

Two of the first friends we were lucky enough to find in those early days were a garage owner and his wife. He had done his best to make Sue's very ancient 'Dyane' roadworthy and now he came up trumps with a reliable little car for me. He brought it to the house on the Satur-day, let me try it and then I drove him back to the garage a couple of hours later. Such an honest and genuine person, I was able to recommend him to so many people over the ensuing years. It was four months after buying the car that I noticed excessive wear on the edge of both front tyres and had popped into his garage on my way to work. 'Oh la la!' was the reaction. I was to leave the car with him for the day, take a courtesy car and return in the evening. At the end of the day, my car had two new tyres and in reply to my question of 'combien je vous dois?' (How much do I owe you) the answer was 'Rien!' (Nothing), I should have done my job better before selling it to you! How could anyone not recommend such a rare, honest, second-hand car salesman to others?!

Accommodation was to be in the medical room at the college which doubled-up as a very full stationery store. Lunch would be in the school canteen and as for breakfast and evening meal 'débrouillez-vous' (cope by yourself) said Monsieur le Principal when I arrived at 7.50am. 'Here's your timetable, 6 different classes through the week'. 'What do I teach?' 'That's up to you, you're the teacher and your first lesson is in 10 minutes'. 'Is there a course book I can have?' 'Your colleagues will be in at break time, they'll lend you one.' So there I was, a foreigner to everyone in the school, entrusted with twenty-two 11 and 12 year-olds, now standing to attention and facing me. No one had asked me to prove my identity and I had no guidelines as to what I should be doing with these young people – who were now eyeing-me up with a look that belied a mixture of curiosity and apprehension. I decided there would be no word of French spoken. 'Use the Direct Method' I told myself. 'Good Morning, please sit down. My name is Mr Holding', accentuating the 'H', 'and I am replacing Madame Dupont this week, who is sick'. I showed them the piece of folded card on which I had printed my name in large letters and asked them to do the same, writing their first name on a piece of folded paper and placing it on their desk, facing it in my direction. Whilst they were doing that, I borrowed a pupil's text book and discovered for the first time what a French course book looked like! It proved to be very attractive and colourful and the class representative indicated what they had been studying – the Present tenses, 'le présent simple' and 'le présent progressif'.

So that's where we started; 'Football', I said. 'I play football' said one child. 'I am playing football' said another. 'I am playing football tonight!' said a third – 'Ah, very good, that's the future tense', I said. 'Ah Non, Monsieur, Madame told us we do the future tense next year and you have to use "will", I will play football!, that's the future she said' 'Yes, that's true, but we can also say I am playing football tonight'. 'Madame is a very good teacher, we like her'. So, already, in French, I had to defend myself, and to convince them that I too could speak English correctly! 'Yes, good, I am sure that Madame is an excellent teacher but I have been speaking in English for quite a long time now and I don't make many mistakes; I assure you that the easiest way to express the future is to use 'le présent progressif' with a time-marker – that's what English people do!'. The continued looks of incredulity and even of antagonism meant I had to work hard to rescue my very first lesson in France! On the blackboard I wrote 'this afternoon', 'tonight', 'tomorrow', 'on Saturday', 'next week', 'next year'...and stuck to the present continuous 'I am eating spaghetti, I am swimming, I am going to the cinema...' and every now and then, pointing to the blackboard. After a while, I congratulated them and was able to say 'tell Madame how an Englishman had been impressed by the way they used the future so convincingly in English' – but would I be reprimanded for trying to teach next year's syllabus! I felt like a new, inexperienced teacher again and was happy to meet my fellow English teachers at break time...But not they to meet me! When I asked if I could sit-in in one of their lessons to see how things were done in France, the answer was unequivocally 'Ah Non! Je suis mâitre dans ma classe, si vous avez des problèmes adressez-vous à l'inspecteur'. (I alone am master in my classroom; if you have a problem consult the inspector.) Obviously, I was seen as a threat, someone who might criticise their command of English!

Well, was there a Head of Department who could guide me? 'Non, non, we are all equal; no one is above anyone else. We all follow "le programme"; you must do the same. Buy the teacher's guide to the course book! But I'm only here for the week and the next school might not use the same publisher! The gallic shrug... I thought back to my Deputy Head days when I'd insisted that Heads of Department provide a source of ready-made work and activities for use by supply teachers when regular teachers were absent; and where the same Head of Department would welcome and look after the supply teacher!

Lunch was the next highlight of my first teaching day in France. Teachers did not sit with the pupils (too noisy!) but were served apart in a quiet annexe of the dining room. This too, was different to County Durham where a salad or a sandwich with the pupils had been hastily consumed before rushing off to a meeting or a 'lunchtime activity'. Instead, a leisurely, four-course 'déjeuner' of cold leeks and boiled eggs à la vinaigrette, chicken and chips, a piece of Camembert followed by a yoghurt. Copious amounts of bread and bottles of 'vin ordinaire'; (all alcohol was banned in school premises in Durham!)

Somehow, afternoon lessons were faced in a more relaxed state after such a civilized break in the middle of the day! Lessons finished promptly at 5.30pm and very quickly the school premises emptied. No after-school activities here – for pupils or staff! The Head went off to his accommodation provided free of charge within the school, as is the case throughout France and I was left to my store cupboard cum infirmary to reflect on the experiences of the day. I decided to go for a walk and to explore this little coastal town.

Not far from the school I came across a charming little restaurant called 'La Porte Verte'. Aha! 6.30pm, I could get something to eat. I tried to push the door, only to find that it was locked. Then I realised that it was a Monday, and many shops and restaurants are closed on a Monday in France. Ah well, I'd get something from the little supermarket I'd spotted just down the road. And then, a noise above my head as a window was thrown open. 'We are clozed, come back at 8 o'clock when we are hopen' – in reasonably well pronounced English! 'How did you know I was English?' I enquired. 'Only the English eat at this time of the day!'. I did return a little after 8pm, was the only customer all evening, but what a meal! and I discovered a new wine – the 'Fiefs Vendéens', wonderful! And I slept very well in my little box room.

Between trying the restaurant door and enjoying my supper, I had been to the supermarket to buy the necessary croissants and coffee for breakfast and had spotted some intriguing self-heating, instant meals! This, I thought, could be helpful for tomorrow's evening meal; I couldn't after all, afford to eat in a restaurant every night on my salary...I chose a 'boeuf bourguignon' (beef with carrots cooked in a wine sauce). If the meal at the 'Green Door' had been excellent, the first meal in my paper store was one of the worst I have ever eaten – before or since. I followed the instructions carefully and pulled the red string sticking out of the aluminium foil wrapping. Immediately, there was a hissing sound, smoke and steam and a very hot meal indeed appeared when I tore back the lid. Chemicals therein, once mixed together had heated-up foul-tasting pieces of gristly meat and it certainly had a 'chemical' flavour to it; an experience not to be repeated! For the other two nights I was invited to colleagues' houses to eat and this first week of work was completed reasonably happily. On the Friday I received details of my next 'mission' which was to replace another sick colleague in yet another small town. Here again, it was far from home and this time I would be able to sleep in...the medical room for 3 weeks this time! But this time, I vowed to take a camping stove and other items to make life more comfortable. After those three weeks I was sent to another collège in yet another small town until the end of the school year, but this time, not too far from home so at least I could return home every evening – which was a real bonus. I must admit that life as a teacher in France was like a fairy tale when compared to teaching conditions in the UK in those days. French teachers were only required to be on the school premises when they were actually teaching and at all other times during the week they could do whatever they wanted! How different from the life of an over-worked, over-stressed teacher in the UK! My English colleagues had to be at school every day, for the whole of the day and if they had any 'free' periods, it was more than likely that they would lose them in order to cover for an absent colleague, thereby losing valuable preparation or marking time which then had to be done at home in the evening. In France, planned absences are covered by Maitres-Auxiliares and unplanned absences mean that the pupils have to go into 'étude' – supervised study – where prefects (usually university students work part-time as prefects to earn a bit of money to help with their studies). The pupils have to sit in silence and do their homework or read a book. In the meantime, teachers who were not down to teach could be at home, working in the staffroom preparing lessons or could nip down to the local bar (for a coffee, of course!). Some colleagues are able to negotiate a timetable where they are free on a Friday afternoon or a Monday morning, thereby extending their weekend, or ask not to work on market day or the chosen day for the weekly visit to the 'coiffeur'!

French teachers also have a more relaxed dress code – like the pupils. No uniforms here with jeans, sweatshirt and trainers being the order of the day for most children – and often for the staff; but the French do seem to have the knack of appearing smart with the most casual of clothes! In Durham, as Deputy Head, one of my daily routines was to stand in the entrance hall every morning to welcome the staff as they arrived – and to invite any male teachers without a tie to return home and dress correctly! In France, to start with, I always wore a tie (old habits die hard and I'd worn a tie every day ever since my own primary school days!) But I soon got tired of constant remarks from colleagues who wanted to know if I was getting married today or if I was looking for promotion or 'was I being inspected today?' June, and the end of the school year soon arrived but during those six months so much had happened! Sue had completed her contract as a Language Assistant and I'd survived my time as a 'Kleenex'. We'd realised that Natalie and Justin didn't need to continue in their college as the 'section bilingue' wasn't at all 'bilingual' and attending a more local collège would mean they could stay in bed a bit longer every morning, be home sooner – and have their Dad around as I'd already received a half-time contract as MA at that college for the whole of the next academic year! The other half-time was to be as an MA at a lycée (6th form college) in Niort.

6

Back to the Land

Our first six months, then, had been dominated by
schooling and work but we hadn't forgotten our primary
reason for wanting to live here – to become 'des paysans'!
As the climate here is so different to that in the North
of England, we decided it would be best to see what our
neighbours did and when, garden-wise. By the end of
January they had already sown garlic, shallots, peas and
broad beans but not parsnips as they'd never seen or
tasted those! And it was true that you never saw any in
the shops or in the market! We had had catching-up to
do – especially as the plot of land we'd decided would
become our 'potager' was still a field and had been left

rough-ploughed. The soil was very red, very heavy and very hard to work. It also didn't hold moisture very well and was in dire need of being limed and nourished with organic matter. It was also unfenced and unprotected from the prevailing Westerly winds.

Again, the neighbours were great. One of the elderly couple's sons came across one morning very excited and saying that his parents needed me *right now*. When I got there, on display in their yard was a very ancient 'motoc-ulteur' – a sort of small tractor for walking behind, with various accessories! The machine was now too heavy and clumsy for Monsieur to operate and 'would I like it for a petit prix'? Of course I would! It consisted of a 2-stroke engine fixed onto a chassis with two tractor wheels, behind which one could attach plough or harrow. There was also a home-made trailer which had been very cleverly constructed in such a way that it could be lengthened and widened to carry several bales of hay or a 'stère' (1 cubic metre) or two of wood; and there was even a power (pto) attachment which would turn a vicious-looking, unprotected circular saw via a long drive belt. The lot came with its original bill of sale of 3,691 francs dating from 1965 (£369), and this was the price asked for now, and duly paid. A real peasant small-holder's workhorse! It had been Monsieur's workhorse and now it would be mine. I did learn to become its master over the next few years but I was always concerned that it would eventually get the better of me and maim me for life as it had no safety features!

Anyway, it did enable me to turn over a large patch of garden and to plough-in sheep manure before rotavating the whole with the small tiller I'd brought from the UK. I proudly sowed Petit Provençal peas for the first time, garlic, shallots, broad beans and even potatoes – not King Edwards' but 'Charlotte' and 'Rosabel' – all unknown to me but I felt it was best to do what the neighbours recommended!

The crops certainly seemed to grow quickly and we were quite happy to be eating peas and broad beans in April. But then May brought a first problem. While soiling-up the potatoes I spotted a few unknown orange grubs on the underside of some of the leaves; they were obviously enjoying a feast as the leaves were disappearing at an alarming rate and one or two plants had been completely stripped! And then I saw what had obviously laid the yellow eggs from which had hatched these orange grubs – yellow and black striped beetles. I'd never come across them before but I remembered having seen posters with pictures of them in police stations back in the UK as a child – Colorado Beetles! Should I contact the Gendarmerie? I knew that's what you had to do in the UK. I took one round to Paul and showed him. 'Ah oui, un doryphore'. Should I take it to the Gendarmes? 'Uh? Pourquoi?' 'Well, they're eating my potatoes'! 'The gendarmes aren't interested in your potatoes – or in your insects! We get 'doryphores' here every year; you have to treat your plants'. 'No, I'm organic; no pesticides'. 'Well, you'll get no potatoes then'. I went back to my garden and painstakingly squashed every beetle, grub and egg I could find – and did the same at least once a day for weeks on end!

It had always been an ambition (of course!) to grow a few vines and I asked Paul if he'd let me have some cuttings. 'Yes, but you need the Mayor's permission to plant vines.' 'Monsieur le Maire, can I have your permission to plant some vine cuttings?' 'Yes, but I'm not sure what the quota you are allowed to plant is, so you'd better telephone the Préfecture'. 'Préfecture des Deux-Sèvres. Bonjour'. No, not Bonjour; there never is a 'bonjour' with French Administration 'Service viticole svp'. 'Service viticole, j'écoute'. 'Bonjour Madame, excusez-moi de vous déranger, recently arrived in the County from the Royaume Uni would it be possible for me to plant my quota of vine cuttings in my garden please?' 'No you may not plant vines'. 'Oh, why, I thought everyone had the right to a few cuttings; is it because I'm English?' 'No, nobody is allowed to plant vines any more – or to dig them up without our permission (!) either'. 'Oh, but it's only so that I can achieve a dream of making a bit of our own wine for our own consumption on our self-sufficient smallholding, as do our neighbours.' 'Non, there is an overproduction of wine in France, donc c'est comme ça.' (so that's how it is) 'Oh, but can I plant cauliflowers then?' 'Yes of course!' 'But I thought there was an overproduction of cauliflowers in France – the farmers in Brittany are tipping them onto the road and driving over them with their tractors!' The line went dead and I could imagine the Préfecture representative doing her gallic shrug and muttering the inevitable 'ils sont tous fous ces anglais...'

Later that day I popped in to see Thérèse. 'Ah Thérèse, Paul tells me you planted your new little vineyard just a couple of years ago; did you have to get permission?' The answer was: 'I think it's going to rain this evening, do you think you could take me to the cemetery at Tessé before it does? I need to clean a tombstone'. Obviously, the way forward was just to do things discreetly, and keep well-in with the neighbours so that they didn't report you to the Mairie.

I did indeed take her to the cemetery and when I looked at the headstone I saw that it was hers! There was her name, that of her husband's and their dates of birth! All that was missing were the dates of death! It shocked me, but why? Why not be ready and save the children from having to cope with the administrative tasks linked to a death? Apparently, this kind of provision is quite common in rural France. Many homes around here even have their own family graveyard in the garden; a practice which dates back to religious intolerance of Protestants and the impossibility for them to be buried in Catholic ground. It must make selling a house difficult however! We were integrating, little by little, into the regular life of the village. We were invited as a family to join Lucienne for her birthday party with all of her extended family at the end of January. Another marathon meal of home-made produce to which had been added free foods collected and preserved over the months. And it was during this meal that we were accorded a heart-warming honour when Lucienne volunteered that she and her husband had been thinking of moving out of Le Sauvage in the near future as they felt increasingly isolated. 'I was born in the village; then there were 20 families or more; now there's only the Vriets. But since you've come you have brought new life and if you're really going to stay, we think we shall!' What a compliment! We felt really touched that a French country family should appreci-ate the arrival of an English family to the extent that they wanted to share their adventure! But there was more when I asked Paul, who was an elected member of the 'Conseil Municipal' (Parish Council) if they had appointed a new 'cantonnier' yet. The cantonnier is the mayor's handyman who maintains the hedges, verges and green spaces in good order. 'Oh pas encore, there are two applicants – Jean-Marc from Pioussay, 4 kms away and a Portuguese man from another village but we don't want any foreigners here!' Odd to think that we were longer seen as being 'foreign'!

Another memorable occasion spent with neighbours during those first few months was the first 'oven day' to which we were invited. Paul's old baker's oven, situated just across the road from our house, was to be fired-up and family, friends and neighbours were invited to prepare suitable dishes for cooking or baking therein. Such ovens were to be found in all the hamlets and villages around, each belonging to a particular family but use of which was shared between several families – originally once a week for the baking of the week's bread supply. In those days the loaves were large 'pain de campagne' and nothing to do with the ubiquitous white 'baguettes' which everyone seems to buy these days – and which go stale in the same day! Most of these ovens have now fallen into extreme disrepair if not disappeared completely to make way for a garage or other new structure but this one was regularly used by our dear neighbours. Paul explained that we couldn't bake bread this time as the oven hadn't been lit for a few months and bread required a very high temperature which could cause the brick lining to crack if the fire was stoked-up too high too quickly. You can bring pizzas, quiches, stuffed tomatoes, roasts, pâtés, terrines, fruit tarts or even try your hand at the local 'fromager' – a soft, cake-like bread mixture with goat's cheese incorporated in a pastry case with a much blackened, burned top to it. The black crust can make the result taste bitter but the cheese-based filling (which doesn't taste of cheese!) makes the cake moist. It's mostly eaten at aperitif-time – in large chunks...

Obviously, such occasions are excuses for tasting everyone else's dishes and sharing unreasonable amounts of wine while sitting or lounging in the road around the oven before taking the culinary delights home to be put into the freezer. How decadent – but how civilized at the same time! No particular event has to be celebrated – just the fact that crops from the garden or collected from the wild have become available; or that it was time to kill the pig or a young goatling (in the Spring and roasted with green garlic – yummy...)

The oven itself – a stone structure measuring some 2 or 3m square, 2m high with a sloping tiled roof – consists of a circular dome of small red bricks set within with an iron door at the front. Faggots – bundles of hornbeam branches are thrown in and lit with the door left open (there is no internal vent). An hour or two later, once the fire has died-down, the inside temperature is tested – not with a thermometer, but usually by throwing a handful of flour into it and judging how quickly this bursts into flames! Once deemed to be at the correct temperature, the embers are pushed to the sides and the prepared dishes placed onto the hot bricks. Again, this is quite an art deciding which dishes need greater heat which are then placed further to the back while pizzas and fruit tarts are placed nearer to the door. The results are fantastic – such tasty food!

7

A Secret Policeman, a General and a New Recruit

During these early months we also had to start coping with further aspects of the to-be-feared French Administration. We needed Health cover and Family Allowance and we were determined to add French nationality to our British in order to show our commitment to becoming more European. In no way did we want to be seen as English living an English way of life in France but this didn't mean renouncing our past or those aspects of Britishness which we held so dear; we wanted to add Frenchness in order to make our lives richer.

The French Social Service system turned out to be very

efficient and generous to us – if slow and cumbersome. As a teacher – a 'fonctionnaire' I was to pay 2.5% of my monthly salary in order to get 100% cover for myself, wife and three children with any up-front payments for visits to the doctor, for x-rays, hospitalisation being immediately refunded fully. The health care from day one was faultless and whenever there was a health inspection for one of the children at school, Sue or I were required, by law, to be present with a paid day off work being automatically granted. The only problem was in trying to understand why so many drugs and medicines were given to treat a common cold or other minor ailment when in the UK the doctor had always said 'go home, stay warm, it'll get better' and perhaps recommended a paracetamol or two!

Another impressive aspect of the Health Service was that all registered workers in France have the opportunity of having a complete health check every few years. Both Sue and I took advantage of this and spent half a day at the Health Centre in Niort with 20 or so other people. After all imaginable tests had been carried out we were individually interviewed by the duty doctor who analysed all of the test results. In my case, all was well until he asked me how much I drank. 'Oh, I have my bottle of red every day, just like our French neighbour does.' 'That's a bit near the limit isn't it?' was the reply.

'You mean it's not enough?' I offered. 'I suppose this is British humour', he said. 'In France you remain master of your body and I can only advise you to drink no more than 3 glasses of wine per day...Concentrate on drinking less, but of good quality; good red wine, especially from the Bordeaux region is good for the cardio-vascular system. Most importantly, avoid wine sold in plastic bottles as they contain hardly any grape juice and lots of chemicals.' Wise advice; certainly, over the years we have learned to appreciate different wines – and it's not a case of wine snobbery, but of an educated palate!

The Family Allowance section or 'CAF'(Caisse d'Allocation Familiale) was also very generous. Having three children made us a 'famille nombreuse' and as our income was so low we were immediately granted (in 1990) a monthly allowance of £256 on top of a salary of £970. We also qualified for reduced rail travel, a grant for sanitation and insulation work on the house as well as a very low interest loan for house improvements. Life was a struggle after giving up such a well-paid job in the UK but it did teach the value of money and good household-accounting to the children!

We approached the Mairie with a view to applying for French nationality – they were really excited as this was a new experience for them – and there again, having three children would reduce the waiting period from five years to two if all went well. Full birth certificates for ourselves, the children and our own parents had to be translated into French by a sworn official translator together with marriage certificate, copies of police records and a rather large file sent to the Prefecture in Niort.

The first consequence of this request, a few weeks' later, was a surprise visit by a gentleman who was 'just passing by'. (Nobody 'passes-by' here, the road doesn't lead anywhere!) He turned out to be an 'Inspecteur Géneral' of the 'Renseignements Géneraux' (the equivalent of MI6), who stayed quite some time. We were subjected to a barrage of questions concerning our daily lives, our origins, and our knowledge of our neighbours and about matters concerning France in general: Could we produce a local newspaper and why did we want to change nationality anyway? All must have gone very well as after a couple of hours and a couple of malt whiskies he went on his way, inviting us to go and listen to a choir he sang in at a concert the following week! He also left us his visiting card saying 'if you have any problems in France, don't hesitate to ring me'! This, I carefully placed in my driving licence knowing that such a contact could only be useful one day...which it proved to be when, during a roadside spot-check some months later I had to negotiate wriggling out of a fine for a somewhat smooth tyre! The gendarme who found the folded card in the licence immediately stiffened and muttered 'roulez' (on your way!).

The CAF grant and cheap loan, together with a bank loan we'd been able to negotiate as a result of a guaranteed, ongoing, job (known as a CDI – 'un contrat de durée indéterminé' as opposed to a CDD (a contract for a defined period of time) enabled us to employ builders straight away. They turned out to be a very impressive team indeed, turning up at 6.30am every morning and working non-stop until lunchtime when they would disappear until 2.30pm. All cups of tea were refused (memories of English tradesmen requiring 'a wet' every hour was a thing of the past!) but they were grateful for 'un petit café' before setting-to and 'un apéritif' at 7.00pm was more or less expected – and this had to be pineau or pastis! It was a mystery to us how they managed to find the energy to work through the afternoons after such a long lunch break, which presumably included drinking wine.

Even today, the average break for lunch for workers in France is 2hours 40 minutes and the 'déjeuner' remains the main meal of the day, being considered as important for the opportunity it offers to strengthen family relationships as well as for the consuming of food. Long may it last!

The stable was quickly transformed into a sitting room, above which we created four bedrooms and a bathroom – and one daughter, at least, was happy and proud at last to have her own private domain!

During that first year we also realised that there was quite a bit of local interest in learning to speak English in the area and, encouraged by different sources, Sue and I decided that we could start up evening classes for small groups of adults in four local towns. It proved to be too complicated for tax purposes to be self-employed whilst also working for the State but in France there is a system where registered associations can employ who they wish and deal with all of the heavy administrative require-ments, including funding the 'charges sociales'. These evening sessions for local bank managers, notaires, bakers, shopkeepers and retired ladies proved to be great fun for both them and for us – although some of the students sometimes came with a strange attitude to a classroom situation! 'Tell the group what your hobbies are'; 'No, don't ask me questions, I've just come to listen and learn'!! or, 'Can you describe your house?'; 'It is none of your business'! But these sessions certainly enabled us to integrate very fully into local society.

One early problem, however, was how to impose our wish that in a class everyone should be equal and that if we were able to establish a happy and supportive environment people would learn more easily with con-fidence. We suggested that as in English there was only one form of 'you', whereas in French there was 'vous' and its more familiar version 'tu' used when addressing a child, close friends or God (!) we should just use 'tu'. This was a deliberate move as there is nothing worse in a staff meeting, for instance, when the Head addresses some people by 'tu' and others by 'vous', leaving some people feeling favoured with others being kept at a distance! On the whole this was accepted but the French do have a strong sense of hierarchy and when we would meet some of the 'students' in the street they would immediately revert back to 'vous'.

Knowing when you can change from the formal 'vous' to the more familiar 'tu' remains a problem. When can you address someone you have 'vous-voyed' for some time with 'tu'? sometimes it just slips out, naturally, and it seems to be accepted; sometimes you can suggest to someone that you'd like to be 'tu-toyed' but often the reply is 'oh, I wouldn't like that, it would be seen as a lack of respect towards you – in the way that a gendarme will address someone he's just stopped for a traffic offence with 'tu' in order to reinforce his authority over that person (which he's not supposed to do).

The ultimate, classic, put-down if you don't wish to be 'tu-toyed' is to reply 'je ne me souviens pas que nous avons élevé des cochons ensemble' (I don't remember having raised pigs with you!).

One extreme example of a somewhat 'silly' situation was a few years' later when we welcomed a comprehensive school Head from the UK for a joint educational project to the lycée in France where I was working. The UK head had introduced himself to me as 'Paul' but when I sat in on their meeting I found myself saying 'tu' to Paul and 'vous' to Mr le Proviseur; a bizarre situation! Our 2-nation project proved eventually to be extremely successful, with an entire class of my French students being able to spend a whole month in the UK studying the origins of the Industrial Revolution in English while an equivalent number of British students were able to spend a month based in our lycée studying the local economy.

At a final evening celebratory party the French Head was heard to announce: 'This project has been a success, although it disrupted our daily school life somewhat. I would like to thank the Rectorat for granting us permission to realise the project, the County Council for our share of the funding and the families for allowing the British students into their homes; and in view of the numerous out-of-school visits I would particularly like to thank the catering staff for providing so many packed lunches'. The British Head replied: 'I would like to thank the teachers involved in the project, so ably led by an inspired coordinator. The project has had a huge educational impact on our curriculum and our school life in general. Our students have worked hard and have been so motivated that we look forward to excellent results in the forthcoming public exams' 'Vive la différence!'?

It was also during this preparatory meeting that I was able to finally comprehend the different vision of the role of a head of school in the two countries. The Proviseur was proudly able to say that he was 1) the representative of the State; 2) that he was the guarantor of the establishment's budget: 3) that he was responsible for the discipline and punctuality of students and the teaching and ancillary staff and the smooth day-to-day running of the establishment; 'C'est tout'! (Nothing else) 'But what about team-building of teachers, the quality of the learning experience received by the students and what happens in the classroom?' 'Not my affair' was the reply, 'that's the role of the inspectors'. The fact that a teacher, on average, is inspected once every 4 to 7 years can only mean that there may be some progress to be made in this domain!

Sue and I continued with evening classes for a couple of years and through them Sue was invited to organise English activities in several local Primary Schools – which she loved. She made quite a hit with the children and whenever she met one of them in the street they would instantly beam and say ''Ello Madame 'Olding, 'ow harre you?'! – very difficult to pronounce, those 'h's'!

I taught less and less evening classes as I had to prepare myself for the Capès exam and this included attending lessons once a week at Poitiers university. Here, we did translation and learned how to do a 'commentaire' or 'explication' of a text – a literary analysis of just about every word in an extract from a literary work – which students who have not been used to the philosophy of Descartes can find quite difficult. I was quite pleased when I got my first piece of work back as I'd got an 8. 'Oh, 8 out of 10, that's not bad', I said. 'Ah non, Monsieur, 8 sur 20, mais c'est très bien!' The thinking behind marking in France really seemed to be to mark down as much as possible rather than marking to encourage. 'Sanction what they don't know rather than value what they do know!'. I began to feel that I really was useless! When it came to the actual exams in February 1993 I got a 6 out of 20! And the last person to scrape through got 5.5! Getting through the written exam, however, meant that you were 'admissible' and could go on to the oral exam a couple of months later in Paris.

I actually looked forward to the oral exam. I thought it would be an enriching experience to be faced by a board of experienced, high-flying colleagues and that we would have the opportunity to discuss different teaching techniques as the exam was to be based on an actual lesson situation.

After a sleepless night in the cheapest, and very sleazy, hotel I could find nearest to the 'Défense' where the exam was to take place, I presented my 'carte de séjour' (residence permit) at the door to the secretary at 8.00am and was ushered into a room already full of nervous candidates to hear the briefing. The Chief Examiner told us that we would have two hours of preparation on a document which was then to be described in English, commented on in English and around which a lesson plan was then to be built and put forward in French. ID had to be shown again as we entered the preparation room and we set-to. My document turned out to be a cartoon picture of a few bedraggled hens and cocks on a rugby field with the title 'Sport and the French' and the caption 'This chapter won't take long, dear readers, as we all know what a set of cheaters and back-stabbers the French are in sport'; it had been taken from a book written by a certain Denise Thatcher!

I really didn't know how to react; the document was such a shock. How could I spend the next two hours working on a lesson support which I could never use? I was really disappointed but had no choice but to do my best. I started by trying to describe the document in the richest language possible to impress the Board and, at the same time, prepare an apologia as to why I found it unsuitable and then decide how anyone could use it with a class of 15 year-olds.

The time to go before 'le jury' couldn't come quickly enough, and when I was accompanied out put on a brave face and smilingly said 'Bonjour M'sieur, Dames' as I faced the jury of three. Their heads looked-up, unsmilingly and the reply was 'carte d'identité et convocation'. I later found out that apparently, smiling was off the menu as this could be seen as favouritism and encouraging one candidate over another and the fact that I'd shown ID to get in and out of the preparation room and had been accompanied to the jury room didn't seem to count! The three members of the jury sat slightly apart from each other at individual desks on a dais and a small table and chair facing them some 5 metres away was indicated to me by Monsieur le Président du Jury, in silence.

'Commencez' (begin), I was told, and I immediately explained that given my origins I didn't feel that I would ever want to insult any French pupils by using a document which accused the French of being cheats and lacking in fair play. Bowed heads and silence was the reaction, so I continued by admitting that the document was 'tongue-in-cheek' and could be seen to be humorous to some readers – but perhaps not teenagers. Again, no reaction so I launched into my prepared description and analysis. Once the allotted time for this part of the exam had been reached, the president looked up and with an unpleasant smile said 'maintenant, en français, votre cours (now let's hear your lesson plan in French), but first of all let us hear what your definition of humour is.' I heard myself saying 'I don't suppose it's the same as yours; English humour is not always understood or appreciated in other cultures and I do try to judge how it may be badly taken at face value in certain circumstances so I will refrain from trying to be humorous at this particular moment'. That actually elicited a discreet smile from one of the lady examiners but I knew I was sailing close to the wind! I felt more and more depressed; After 23 years of teaching including 3 in France, of spending all of my spare time and energy into preparing for the exam and building myself up to be tested by who I thought were going to be interesting experts who were going to stimulate me with their teaching techniques and encouraging ideas, here I was facing three antagonistic 'Agrégés' – the so-called elite of the French teaching profession who have had the good fortune to have been successful in the highly selective competitive exam for teachers known as the 'Agrégation'. Agrégés are of course paid much more, teach far less hours (which seems wrong to me because if you're an excellent teacher perhaps you should teach more and spread your expertise!), and never teach in difficult schools where their skills could be put to better purpose! (this is left to newly-appointed, inexperienced teachers in their first posting!). In truth, agrégés are not necessarily good teachers but simply people expert in some aspect of language or literature rather than in teaching techniques.

Each member of the jury was allowed to ask me one question and there was never any further discussion concerning my answers and, of course, no comment was volunteered about anything; I left the room thoroughly disheartened, convinced that all had been lost. On the way out I came across two candidates who were crying and a third who was shouting 'who do they think they are just trying to treat us as if we know nothing...'

In those days, every household had a 'minitel' provided by France Telecom and this was a sort of mini primitive computer on which you could find someone's phone number, consult your bank account, see what the weather was going to be like or consult the different departments of French Administration, etc. Armed with a secret pass number I was able to consult the list of those lucky enough to have 'passed' the Capès exam. I had – but only just and that meant I would become 'titulaire' (incumbent) of a post and would have employment for the rest of my working life; such relief! I was to present myself for my probationary year at the nearest lycée, the Lycée Général André Theuriet and the first thing I did was to establish in which battles this particular general had distinguished himself – only to find out that André

Theuriet had been a minor 19th century novelist and that the 'general' referred to the fact that the lycée was not a technical or a vocational one, just a 'general' lycée!

Just before the results of the Capès were made public we received an official letter stating that our application to become French citizens had been accepted and that our names had been published in the 'Journal Officiel' – the official daily bulletin of the Assemblée Nationale. With pride we went to the Marie to receive our 'Carte d'Identité' and the 'Livret de Famille'. This is the family record book given to every couple when they marry and into which all births and deaths are recorded. There were a few changes to our names. When you apply to become French citizens, you are invited to 'francicise' your surname and first names, or adopt more French names. The family name remained 'Holding' as there are Holdings in France (although we do sometimes receive phone calls asking us what sort of Holding [business] we run!), my suggestion to turn Garry into Gilles was made fun of by Sue and the children, so I remained Garry – which does sound OK in French. Sue became 'Suzanne' and the two boys' names were French anyway but poor old Natalie was persuaded to use the French spelling of 'Nathalie' and she's regretted it ever since...So now we were French and all we still had to do was to become paysans!

Then came another official letter, this time from the

Ministry of Defence. 'Following your successful request to become a French citizen we require you to report to the barracks in Poitiers where arrangements will be made for you to satisfy national service requirements...' That was something I hadn't counted on! After some thought I decided 'why not?' Why not support my new country of adoption by serving under the colours for twelve months? Perhaps I could learn to drive a tank or become a waiter in the Officer's Mess – in Tahiti! But then, the salary was so low that it wouldn't be sufficient to repay our new bank loan and it was eventually decided that I could be dispensed – but was considered apt to be placed on the Reserve list until the age of 50! I still carry my French National Service card today! By the time Richard and Justin reached National Service age, French youths were given the choice of doing the traditional army service, civic service or, if in further education, being exempted – which is what they chose.

8

Monsieur le Proviseur and Monsieur le Président

On the home farm front, we'd bought a young Jersey heifer almost straight away as well as a couple of newly-weaned pigs and four populated beehives to add to the different fowl and all of this meant that going out to work had been proving to be more and more difficult when there were animals to be looked after. Sue, in particular, wanted to revert to being the farmer with me being the farmer's husband! – as had been the case in the UK; and this had been made possible quite unexpectedly in early 1993. On one memorable winter's evening there was a very distressed and animated Joel at the door; his mother had collapsed in a chair, his father was having an attack and all of this was because his brother, Gerard had come home drunk on his mobylette and was shouting and threatening to jump on his new watch! We rushed round to the house and while Sue tended to Thérèse and I put myself between Gérard and his father, Pierre – poor old Pierre really did look in a bad way; he'd had a hard life and having two slightly mentally handicapped boys – now men – giving him behavioural problems on a daily basis over the years had visibly taken its toll. All we could do was to persuade Gérard to come home with us, which he did, and once there we gave him bowls of soup and strong coffee and put him to bed in a spare room to sober-up.

Apparently, this was a regular happening. Gérard was more independent than his brother and actually held down a job making wooden crates for cauliflowers and boxes for Camembert cheeses in a local factory but often, after work, he didn't need much persuading to go to a local café for a drink with his mates. He was of very small build, very thin and carried the nickname of Popeye. His fellow work mates delighted in encouraging him to drink too much – and it didn't take much to get him drunk. For this reason, he was often looked after by a foster family in order to give his parents an easier life. Both of the sons had the same legal guardian who looked after their finances but Joel was allowed to stay with his parents. The next morning, a very repentant Gerard went home but he was soon sent back to us with instructions to make himself useful in our garden to thank us for our kindness. When his 'tuteur' (legal guardian) turned-up (mother had summoned him to come and sort her son out!) it was suggested to us that we should consider applying to becoming a foster family for people like Gerard; and it could be a good solution for Gerard to continue to live in the same village as his parents but under our care.

This then proved to be a perfect solution for us too! Sue could become the farmer at home, Gérard could live with us and give a hand with tasks 'chez nous' and 'chez Maman!' The very next day, Sue applied to be 'responsable de famille d'accueil à domicile' (foster family) with the appropriate section of the 'Conseil Général des Deux-Sèvres' (County Council Social Affairs Office). Very soon there was a meeting in our kitchen with Gerard's tutor, the local social worker and the person in charge of foster families for the County. The local Gendarmerie had already been contacted as well as our Maire for background checks and masses of paperwork were gone through.

We had to admit to being quite favourably impressed with the whole business. It was actually very efficient! Sue was asked to choose between looking after children, old people or handicapped people and would be required to attend a course of preparation in the chosen field. As we had Gérard in mind, she opted for handicapped people and very soon she received the required 'Agrément' (Approval) and Gérard moved in. Another step towards becoming French paysans – looking after and being responsible for one in our home!

Although being a 'famille d'accueil' is a huge responsibility, very demanding and sometimes quite wearing, it is also very rewarding and provides moments of great enjoyment and satisfaction. The financial rewards, of course, are not great and Sue received three payments per month: rent, keep and salary, the whole amounting to around 1,200€ before tax, of which only the salary part was taxed. Because we were living a paysan's lifestyle – vegetables, fruit, meat and dairy products, etc, all home-produced and burning locally cut wood, the money she received was a useful complement to my now enhanced salary as 'un professeur cértifié' and we started to live less precariously! We remained a 'famille d'accueil' over the next 20 years – until our retirement, eventually looking after two adults on a permanent basis with the possibility of looking after a third temporarily. We put them in 'Granny's cottage' – which gave them some independence and us, as a family with children, some evening family time together.

After Gérard had moved in with us his elderly parents told us that they had both worked in the lycée where I had been appointed many years ago! Pierre's job had been to fill buckets of water from the school well in the yard and to carry them up to the girls' dormitory every morning for their morning ablutions whilst Thérèse cut up bread for breakfast! There were no dorms by the time I taught there – and no trace of a well either; but the yard was still there! All of the older lycées seem to have been built to the same design as this one – tall buildings around a courtyard of lime trees and during breaks between lessons M le Proviseur would be standing to attention at one of the entrances to ensure that there was no dallying or late-coming!

This supervision also concerned the teaching staff! Any member of staff who had spent too much time at the photocopier, for instance, was cruelly berated; any pupils who ventured into the yard a few seconds before the bell had rung for the end of a lesson were immediately accompanied back and he would berate the guilty member of staff in front of the pupils as well as the pupils themselves; M le Proviseur would then lurk in the corridor, hoping to catch other culprits! The aura of self-importance which some French proviseurs accord themselves can also lead to humorous situations. One teacher of French, habitually late for her first lesson, one morning fell-upon the proviseur awaiting her at the door of the classroom. Quicker than he she blurted out 'Ah M le Proviseur, did you want to see me? Sorry I can't speak now I'm already late for my lesson' and disappeared into the classroom, leaving him 'bouche-bé' (speechless).

Later in the day, when the same teacher was marking work in the staffroom, the proviseur came in to try to berate her again. Quicker than he again, and in front of colleagues she said 'Ah, M Dupont, is it true there's a meeting this evening after school about the forthcoming fête?'. Trying to show his self-importance the reply was 'If you'd addressed your question to M le Proviseur you would have had a reply'! Her quick replique was 'Oh but I would have thought that M le Proviseur would have kept M Dupont informed!'. I tried to calm the situation somewhat by using the correct form of address and asked M le Proviseur a further question about the fête to which his reaction was – silence and a stare. I gave a confused look and eventually he said 'I am ignoring you because you ignored me in the yard this morning'. 'What? Ignored you? I remember quite distinctly going up to you, shaking your hand and wishing you a "good morning"' His response thundered out 'Non, M Holding, c'est moi qui vous a salué en premier; vous m'avez simplement répondu'. 'Oh, were you quicker than me? Sorry'. 'You are a teacher, I am a proviseur; you should have wished me a good morning first'. 'But Monsieur, I am older than you, was a Head before you and I still hold retired Headship status in a member country...'

It really was disappointing to have become part of a system where hierarchy was based on fear of loss of status and dignity rather than on earned respect and also where useful experience counted for far less than simple years of service. This is still true today, including in the Health Service where highly experienced and competent doctors from abroad are trusted to carry out important medical operations on a regular basis but are not rewarded on the same basis as French doctors with less experience but more service to the French system.

In my own case, following my qualification in the Capès exam, I was informed that as a 'new' teacher I would be paid on Scale 1. When I reminded the Rectorat that I had been a qualified teacher for 23 years – and even a Secondary School Deputy Head – I was reminded that my service had not been 'pour La France' and that if I ever wanted to become a proviseur I would need five years of service in France. Well, I didn't want to become a proviseur in France; that role had nothing to do with the quality of teaching and learning and I'd run away from the UK to avoid becoming a full-time administrator. I was enjoying a teacher's life in France; a teacher's life was so less hectic, I liked my colleagues and I especially liked working with most of my classes; and it gave me time to live as a paysan!

My only solution to receive a fair salary was to ask the Rectorat to acknowledge European law and take into account my experience as a qualified teacher in a Member State. The reply was 'we do acknowledge the law but we don't apply it'. Battle-lines were therefore drawn and I had no choice but to seize the 'Tribunal Administratif' in Poitiers and make my case. The services of a TA are available, free of charge, to all French citizens and it will listen to any 'receivable' plea made against the Administration. Of course, this not a quick procedure – anything to do with French administration takes ages and ages.

To make my plea receivable I needed a lawyer to write it; fortunately the teacher's union I was a member of was keen to help and to make jurisprudence. Then I had to furnish proof of my career, and then translate everything into French – or, more precisely, have it translated by a sworn translator appointed by the Court of Appeal in Poitiers. In addition, letters had to be written to our 'Député' (local MP), the Minister for Education, the European Commission, etc, etc. It was months before our dossier was ready.

Eight years later into my new teaching career, standing in the court room in the Tribunal Administratif in Poitiers, I heard Monsieur le President du Tribunal say

'Nous trouvons pour Mr Holding et nous condamnons l'Etat'. Tears trickled down my face and I managed a squeaky 'Je vous remercie, Monsieur le Président' and left in a state of relief and elation. My case had been the eighth to be dealt with on that day and all arguments and counter arguments had taken place beforehand, the public 'hearing' just to give a final opportunity for both parties to make a final statement.

This, however, was not the end. While the wily officials at the Rectorat did not appeal against the judgement, they did ask me if I'd had a contract in the UK. 'Of course' I had replied: 'Ah, so you were "*un contractuel et non un titulaire*"' ('titulaire' means incumbent and 'contractuel' refers to a lower status where the teacher is not on a permanent post). They therefore decided to take into consideration just 70% of my experience, in line with the salary of a 'contractuel' and to pay me accordingly.

They didn't count on my tenacity, however, and I re-seized the TA. One year later, in 2001, the latter gave the judgement 'You will pay Mr Holding in complete accordance with his experience in the UK and in France immediately or you will be fined 500€ per day'. Within a week I received a handsome sum of money and some of our financial difficulties came to a welcome end. The ruling did create jurisprudence and all other teachers from the UK who had made the move to France were able to benefit from it. The case is today used in lessons in the faculty of Law at Poitiers university – where our daughter Natalie just happens to now teach English!!

9

Pigs, Pineau and Planing

My life at that time was certainly very taken-up with the French educative and administrative system in our new adventure but, alongside, we were still striving to become paysans! Full-time teaching in a French lycée certainly offers a lot of free time. Eighteen 45 minute lessons per week (plus preparation and marking time!), few meetings after school and hardly any extra-mural activities fitted in very well with small-scale farming and we bought a couple of weaners in our first year and looked around for a Jersey heifer to rear into a house-cow. We eventually spotted an ad for one not too far away and we had an exciting ride home with her in our Deux-Deuche

(Citroën 2cv)! She certainly fitted in with the family very well and we immediately went up in our neighbours' estimation – cow pats hadn't been seen on the village road for years!

Some months later, when she first came on heat, the artificial inseminator was called in to do the necessary. This, he did and there then followed an embarrassing conversation... 'Voila, c'est fait; what's the number of your cow?'. 'Number? Well we only have one cow, so she's number 1'. 'What, you don't have a number! I'm not allowed to inseminate her without a number!'. 'Oh, sorry, it's a bit late now..., but we did have a herd number in the UK, will that do?' 'Non, we might be living in Europe mais ici c'est la France!' An urgent phone call was made and a somewhat irate official turned up, with lots of 'paperasse' and an ear-tagger – and a few months later 'Mirabelle' gave us a lovely bull calf and lots of milk. The house cow, of course, is the keystone of any self-sufficient smallholding. The two milking times, early morning and late afternoon, set the rhythm for the day's routine and the milk isn't just for drinking. Sue returned to skimming off the cream for butter, making yoghurt and adding rennet to some of the still warm milk to make cheese. Any spare milk, and especially the buttermilk and whey would go straight to the pigs; it's amazing how quickly pigs will fatten on buttermilk and barley flour!

Six months after buying our first couple of weaners, they were ready for killing and a decision had to be made on how they were to be slaughtered – and by whom! In the UK a local friendly butcher had always come to us on a Saturday, and with the Border Collie hiding and growling under his car and our young children keeping their distance, Sue and I had given the necessary help before he took the carcasses away and turned them into chops and joints a few days later. There was no such friendly local butcher near us in France and I hadn't liked the way Paul, our neighbour had dispatched his pig in his yard a couple of months earlier. Then, it had been a swift blow to the pig's head with a heavy hammer before its throat had been cut; but the worst was that the pig was then scorched all over by bundles of burning straw in order to get rid of the many hairy bristles. Paul must have noticed my disapproving look, although I had said nothing, as he was heard to mutter to his colleague in crime 'we'll see how l'Anglais does it when the time comes'.

I toyed with the idea of taking mine to the local abattoir some 12 kilometres away, but when I went there to investigate the possibility and was invited to watch a batch of pigs being slaughtered I quickly decided to find the courage to do the deed myself; well, I had served my apprenticeship in the UK, helping our butcher, and if I did it well, Paul could only be impressed! The abattoir visit was the first time I had seen the industrial killing of animals and it did give me a very uncomfortable, even sickening feeling...at least our pigs (I hope and believe!) had a reasonably happy life and when the day came their death would be as humane as I could make it. What clinched the deal was the notice I spotted on the abattoir wall 'Il est formellement interdit d'abattre chez soi, veaux, cochons, agneaux, chevreaux, et cetera; cependant, il est toléré'!!!!! So it was against the law to kill an animal at home, but a blind eye would be turned as all country folk were expected to kill their own animals at home for home consumption.

I managed to find a local butchers' supplier and bought the necessary tackle – knives, meat saw, gambrel and humane killer (a handgun with a captive bolt) for which I didn't have to have a firearm licence!

The appointed day came and I was very nervy and stressed as I found myself in charge of a village day of entertainment. Sue had heated up gallons of water to near boiling point, Lucienne had brought a large frying pan to collect the blood, some vinegar and a wooden spoon and Paul his strength and his curiosity!

At the door of the sty Sue held Piggy's tail, Paul grabbed it's right ear and I it's left ear and fired the bolt into the victim's forehead. Piggy fell instantly and once I'd inserted the knife deep into its breast, Paul 'pumped' a front leg to make the blood flow out more quickly while Sue caught it in a frying pan and passed it on to Lucienne who added the vinegar and stirred vigorously. All had gone very well according to plan so far, to my great relief; it's strange how one views an animal one has nurtured over a few months as a simple lump of meat in a few seconds and how conversation immediately turns to commenting about the size of future joints and the quantity of black puddings there would be according to the quantity of blood! 'Il est généreux avec son sang' (he's very generous with its blood) offered Lucienne and the passing postman who'd spotted the scene, stopped and offered to lend us his measurer for the black puddings, opening his flies as he approached us! No, it'll be too short said Lucienne, causing great hilarity! Perhaps it was just as well the postman didn't actually show his measurer...!

If Paul had been impressed by the way Piggy had been despatched, he was really impressed when it came to scraping off the hairs and bristles. Instead of burning the carcass with handfuls of flaming straw, we used the UK way which consisted of slowly pouring small quantities of very hot water over areas of the pig and then scraping with the base of a metal candlestick or a small pan lid; the result is clean, shiny, white skin instead of black, charred flesh. Paul was really impressed. I winked at Sue and we both had the warm feeling that we had made another important step into becoming accepted as paysans!

The rest of the job was a doddle; hoisted up on a gambrel hanging from a beam – instead of tied to a ladder – Piggy was slit down, emptied out and cut lengthways into two. The cheeks were minced into the blood and Sue and Lucienne had a good giggle as they teased the mixture with their wet hands through a funnel into lengths of sausage skins (postman size?). We then enjoyed a festive lunch – not pork, of course, but beef 'pot au feu' (see recipe chapter) as you never fancy eating what you're in the process of butchering! – and half a pig was exchanged for a future lamb. Piggy number 2 suffered the same fate later in the day and we then had all the 'cuisine de cochon' to face – twice (see recipe chapter).

Dealing completely with a pig – there's only its tail and its squeak you can't use! – really is challenging, as we had found back in the UK; but here we had to add French recipes to our repertoire also. In the UK, apart from black pudding with oatmeal and cubes of fat added rather than any meat, it had been a question of chops, roasts, Cumberland sausages, pork pie and brawn and sometimes also bacon and gammon. Now it was also to be pâté, rillettes, escalopes, rouelles and rôtis, jambon sec, salted trotters and ears, different sorts of sausages and saucissons and gigouris! At least three day's work!

Recipes for all of these can be found later in the book – plain, salted and smoked!

The next project was to become Sue's speciality – Pineau-making. Pineau is the local aperitif and is what's usually offered when you call in to a neighbour's house. Origins of the drink are unclear but I reckon that as this isn't an area renowned for the quality of its wine, at some point some paysan must have experimented and added a bit of cognac to his wine, and liked what he'd tasted!

We had a vine growing along the whole of the front of the house (une treille) which must have been there for as long as the house had, and it produced small black grapes which weren't really nice to eat. The previous owner had told us that he made his 'vin de la vigne' from it – The recipe for Pineau couldn't be simpler – just freshly pressed grape juice and 'eau de vie' – distilled wine, about 60° proof or more – which has to be added to the juice at a ratio of around 2/3 juice to 1/3 of alcohol to end up with a Pineau at 17°. The problem, of course, is getting hold of the eau de vie as it's not on sale. The only way is to know someone who knows someone else, etc, who can get it from a cognac producer. When wine is distilled for cognac, the first and last parts of the distillate are put aside with only the middle part of the distillate being used in brandy-making; this 'head' or 'tail' of the process is what you need to try and buy for Pineau-making. Until very recently, if you didn't manage to find any eau de vie, you could purchase 90° proof Ethanol from a friendly chemist, but that is also now forbidden...We still have happy memories of making regular visits to different chemists armed with a small bottle in a brown paper bag and asking for the bottle to be filled with alcohol 'for cleaning wounds'; at the end of a year there would be enough for making the year's supply of pineau – and we used 'Dettol' for cleaning wounds!

Sue's first attempt met with approval – and we went up another notch in the paysan stakes... She'd collected the grapes, crushed them through a hand mill, sieved the mush, measured the resulting juice and worked out how much eau de vie to add. No sugar is added – or anything else. Left to settle, the Pineau can then be filtered after a few weeks and bottled. Looking after the vine is very easy, it just needs pruning twice a year – the most important one being in late Winter/early Spring when each sprig has to be cut down to one or two shoots. Sometimes, we also spray with 'bouillie bordelaise', (copper-sulphate) to counteract disease but we've been lucky up to now. As we weren't allowed to plant any vines, we did allow the end of the 'treille' to grow downwards and we then planted the end when it reached soil level – several times (!) so that the 'treille' then went up again and also went along the front of the pigsty and our little cottage next door. Sue now makes at least 60 litres of the stuff each year! Pineau, of course, is not to be confused with 'Pinot' (gris, blanc, noire...) which refers to grape varieties. Our 'treille' variety is Bacco, an old variety which is not planted any more. Pineau should also not be confused with 'piquette' and if this is not poor wine made by adding water to spent lees, it's wine made from adding sugar to poor quality crushed grapes by the locals for their own daily use. The mixture is then allowed to ferment and the result is a fizzy, fruity wine-like drink. Pineau does not ferment – that's the whole idea of adding the eau de vie as this prevents any fermentation from taking place.

We also have learned how to make a whole variety of alcoholic drinks from local produce – not wines à l'anglaise with yeast being added to different fruit and vegetable mixtures, but drinks based on the addition of red wine, sugar and pure alcohol of different degrees mixed with different berries, leaves, flowers and nuts without their being fermented – see later in the book for recipes. The most remarkable of all of these beverages, however, is the home-made 'Gnole' – strong alcohol distilled from apples, peaches and especially, plums. In order to be able to distil, you need to have been a registered farmer at a certain date in the past century! Such farmers were given the right to produce a given quantity of litres each year and the right was passed down through the generations – a practice which has now been stopped; but Paul had that right when we first moved here, and we had lots of plum and peach trees so we came to an arrangement that we'd collect the fruit and he'd make use of his right to make some 'eau de vie de prunes et de pêches'.

Every day, for two months, we collected the two different fruits which we put into two large barrels until they were full to the top. Paul then judged how much sugar should be added – and then informed us that we should have taken the stones out of the peaches as otherwise, if they were distilled, the resulting alcohol would be poisonous! There was nothing else to do but to roll our sleeves up and de-stone every single peach in the barrel.

After a few months, when the mixture in the two barrels was really smelly, Paul went to the Gendarmerie, showed his permit, and obtained a 'laisser-passer' which gave us the permission to transport two barrels of smelly fruit and a barrow-load of oak logs to the 'bruleur', an itinerant distiller, with whom Paul had fixed a time and who had set up camp in a caravan a few kilometres away in the middle of a field. Next to his caravan was his wood-fired still, piles of logs and all around were discarded heaps and heaps of spent fruit – fruit out of which all goodness had been boiled out. The whole area reeked of alcohol and we were met by a jolly, very red-faced 'bruleur' (still operator) – red because of the heat of his fire but, I suspect, that he had the habit of tasting each batch of 'gnole' and that his face was permanently red! Barrels were inspected and unloaded, the logs accepted and we were told to return at a certain time in the evening of the same day.

This we did, and as we approached the caravan another 'client' was slowly walking away from the still towards us and his car ; three laboured paces more or less in a forwards direction, followed by one step backwards, two paces forwards, one backwards and then he fell flat on his back and started immediately to snore very loudly. I was very relieved that he hadn't got to his car! We left him where he was in the grass. Then it was our turn to collect our 'goute', but, of course, we had to taste it first... strong, 65°, giving a burning sensation and with a strong odour of plums for one and of peaches for the second. Quite pleasant but not a patch on cognac! We paid the 'bruleur' and he then insisted on 'paying us un apéro'; we couldn't refuse but I'd already had enough to drink with the 'goute'! We stepped over the peacefully sleeping man and headed for the bruleur's house where we were met by a very garrulous and friendly wife who also had a characteristically red face! No choice in the drinks; men around here drink Pastis – the aniseed-flavoured drink which you dilute with 5 parts of iced water. In this case, we were handed a large dose of Pastis (51°) with 1 part water! I sipped a bit and started asking him questions about his job. It turned out that he'd been a 'bruleur' for many years, having taken over from his father and as the distillation was a seasonal activity he combined this with other farming activities. I asked him about drinking and driving; 'as you work with alcohol all day, every day, do you have any problem with the Gendarmes when they carry out breathalyser controls?' 'Oh no, they allow me 10 or 20% above the limit to compensate for my profession'!!!! I managed to pretend to drink my pastis and poured it into a house plant discreetly; Paul had a second one with the bruleur – and I drove us home.

Wine and drinking alcoholic beverages in general, does play an important part in French life but times are really changing in this domain. Some of the older locals, 'les anciens', still swear by having a shot of 'gnole' even before breakfast, 'une bistouille' to set them up for the day and others like to have a drop in their still-warm coffee cup at the end of a meal – sometimes dipping a sugar-lump into the cup and sucking it ('un canard') but I'm not fond of the flavour and still have bottles of the stuff from over 20 years ago!

Fifty years ago, families drank wine at every meal – children included, although diluted with water. Today, many families will only drink wine at the weekend, choosing the more expensive ones; quality rather than quantity. Paul, our neighbour has always had wine throughout the day – even for breakfast with his Camembert and pâté! And if anyone calls to see him during the day they will be obliged to 'boire un coup'; if they refuse, they offend. If the younger French in the area have lost the habit of drinking every day, this is not the case with many of the waves of ex-pat British moving into the area, however. They seem to get through gallons of the stuff, constantly joke about it and open themselves up to criticism at village fêtes when they remain after the French have gone home and not leaving until they have emptied all of the bottles left unfinished by the French!

But a meal in France still has to include carefully chosen wines to accompany the different dishes or deciding what meal to have can depend on what wine is available! This is one reason why taking a bottle of wine as a gift to a French person who has invited you to lunch or supper is not a good idea. The host will have chosen his or her wines according to what is to be eaten and won't know what to do with the bottle you've taken. 'Does this English person expect me to serve this wine with the meal, or can I keep it for another day?' Much better to take a bouquet of flowers for the lady of the house or a box of English confectionery!

I suppose that becoming a 'famille d'accueil' enabled us to learn the etiquette linked to eating and it was probably the most important step we took in being acknowledged as paysans as we were expected to run our lives in the way the people we fostered were accustomed to; rural France is indeed a 'state of the mind' and rural France does centre around what happens at table. It's not so much the food – although this IS important – but the sharing of the occasions around the table that give cohesion to a family and reinforces friendships is a primordial aspect of French life.

Breakfast has to be a bowl – not for cereal – but for coffee or chocolate and even tea these days, accompanied by bread or perhaps biscottes (rusks) – or croissants and 'pain au chocolat' of course. A cooked breakfast is 'out', as is 'Marmite'! 'Elevenses' do not exist and if you offer a visitor PG tips with milk and sugar at any time you will be rewarded with a perplexed look. If a neighbour visits you at 11.30 in the morning, however, he will expect be offered 'un apéro' such as a pineau or 'un petit jaune' (pastis), Failure to offer an apéro may be seen as being unfriendly...

Lunch is at midday (when the village church bell rings) and if you are driving your car on a country road between noon and 1.00pm, beware of distracted motorists as they're either rushing home to get their lunch or, if out of sector, will be looking for a restaurant and 'le plat du jour'! Lunch, or 'la soupe' as it is referred to around here, could indeed be a soup to start with but will consist of other courses – albeit simple ones. The starter could be just a hard boiled egg with a blob of mayonnaise or a single tomato with vinaigrette. A small amount of goat's cheese melted onto a piece of toast with a lettuce leaf is a local delicacy as is an artichoke heart with vinaigrette but the 'plat de résistance' (the main dish) will always be meat or fish – with no vegetarian option. People I have known asking for a vegetarian meal are usually served with an omelette – with bits of 'lardons' to give flavour! (small cubes of bacon). Sometimes the 'accompanying' vegetables to a main course will be served separately. Then the cheese course will follow, perhaps with lettuce and dressing and then dessert and coffee. Bread and water (or wine) will be constantly available. As a foster family, in our contract, we also had to provide a 'goûter' or 'quatre heures' snack – a piece of fruit tart or bread with chocolate spread with the last meal of the day being the evening meal. This 'repas du soir' usually consisting of perhaps soup again followed by pâté, or pasta, or eggs followed again by cheese and dessert.

All meals around here, of course, are based on what is available from the 'basse cour' (farmyard) or 'potager' and as many of the mostly retired country folk around us – even today – have little income – this is reflected in what they eat. Our immediate neighbour, who has now turned 80 receives 800€ per month pension after a long and hard life on his small (26 hectares) farm. As an 'ancien combattant' (ex soldier) who did National Service in Algeria, he receives an extra 160€ per annum and his wife, as 'farmer's wife', 300€ per month. Were her husband to leave her (it does happen that older retired farmers set-up with younger women!) she would have to survive on a very small income indeed...

We have sometimes shared an unplanned meal with them and these have been very telling of their financial condition. On occasions it has been a question of just potatoes with a piece of butter, 'He doesn't like it when we eat potatoes' – not surprising! At other times it could be cubes of boiled beetroot from a jar with vinegar. 'Oh this beetroot's a bit brown'. Indeed it was, and it tasted foul, but nothing else was forthcoming. I remember calling in on a hot Summer's afternoon when Lucienne was cutting up cubes of bread and placing them into a bowl. 'The dog's not getting much to eat today', I thought to myself. Then she added lumps of sugar, 'Oh, that's a bit better'. Then she added ice cubes onto which she poured red wine...Not for the dog, then, but for me and them. 'Mijot', it's called, and it's very refreshing for 'quatre heures'! But not all of what our dear neighbours prepare to eat is bizarre or unattractive; it's just that so often they seem to produce something out of nearly nothing and certainly nothing is wasted. Who, for instance would think of making cocks' combs into a pâté? or stuffing the skin of a duck's neck with chopped herbs and a little pork fat? Such resourcefulness!

Gerard, the first person we looked after certainly brought his requests for favourite foods and we did try to satisfy him but we did draw the line at 'gigouris' which was finely minced pig skin fried in seasoned red wine and served with mashed potatoes...

He certainly fitted-in well with our chosen lifestyle. Always polite and grateful towards us he was also willing to help with routine animal husbandry and in the 'potager' – but, less on our terms than on his, or rather his mother's! Little by little I lost control of our garden and would come home to find that 'Maman' had told him to dig this up or plant something there. His mother, I suppose, was only trying to 'look after' us and in return we were frequently summoned to help her out – fixing the shower, grape-picking, cutting-up her pig and even picking-up her poor husband, Pierre when he collapsed from a heart attack.

After he'd died in Sue's arms we then had to participate in what all neighbours do when someone dies in a small village; we had to get the body washed and dressed, ready for placing into the coffin at which point the Maire would come and place his seal on the lid. Funeral arrangements for 'Maman' included buying a tin of black paint so that Gerard and his brother could paint their shoes! The village church bell rang 'le glas' and the date of the death was added to that of his birth on the previously prepared gravestone.

After the death of his father, Gerard continued to live with us but he lost his job in the local factory so we had him very full time. This meant he could devote most of his time to his two favourite activities – visiting the local tips to return with 'treasures'; old clothes, pictures, books (he couldn't read!), interestingly-shaped pieces of wood, discarded tools, etc. These visits, he would make on his moped so we bought him a trailer to attach behind it. It really was a matter of pride for him to return home with 'quelque chose d'util'. We had allocated him an outbuilding so that he had somewhere to store these treasures and also somewhere where he could pursue his other preferred activity – planing wood.

His favourite possession was an electric planer and with this he would plane and plane thick chestnut stakes or logs (destined originally for the wood-burning stove) into a variety of imaginative objects from horse-collar-shaped mirror frames to models of working spinning wheels which gave him great pleasure to give to anyone who was interested; a remarkable feat when one remembers he couldn't measure – or see very well through the very thick lenses of his glasses which were always covered with a film of fine sawdust! How many times did I have to rewire his planer after he'd planed over the lead!

We had wonderfully entertaining discussions with him and I think that we really gave him a new dimension to his life, On one occasion he mentioned that he'd been to Paris as a child with an aunt and that he'd really enjoyed himself and that gave us the idea of how we could really reward him for his help around our smallholding. He and I took the train together and had a 2-day trip to the capital and while he enjoyed seeing the Eiffel Tower again his chief interest was in trying to catch pigeons and gathering as many cigarette butts as he could from the pavement! Unfortunately, little by little, 'Maman' tried to be too helpful/interfering and several times a day would come round to check on things – lifting the lids off pans to see what her son would be eating for lunch, complaining that his socks hadn't been correctly darned, etc. Things came to a head when I felt obliged to ban him from using his moped when he returned home one Sunday afternoon quite drunk (not for the first time) having 'fait le tour des copains' (visiting several mates). Mother was furious – who were we to ban her son from his mode of transport? Quiet reasoning was to no avail and she didn't seem to understand that we were, after all, responsible for her son's safety and welfare and thankfully his legal guardian supported us against his mother; but this made her really turn against us and Gerard was placed in another family far away – too far for Mother to be able to interfere in his daily life. Maman then began to show her vindictive side. Two events remain in our minds; the first when she contacted the Maire to inform him that we had tethered our house cow to the well on the hamlet green and she was eating the commune's grass! The second when she again complained to the Maire that Mr Holding's bees had drunk all of the water she had put out for her hens, and that Mr Holding should control his bees better! The fact that a professional bee-keeper had 50 hives in a copse near by was irrelevant!

LIBERTE EGALITE FRATERNITE

10

Life with Bernard

We were then entrusted with a series of men and women for varying periods of time, from weekend breaks from psychiatric hospital to several weeks for people with very confused minds; each individual presenting us with new and different challenges. Eventually we were asked to take on two men on a permanent basis. They didn't know each other but both came to us from unhappy backgrounds.

The first, Jean-Marie, in his late 40's, had actually been beaten by his previous foster family for being clumsy and lazy! Before that, he had spent most of his life in the men's wing of the local psychiatric hospital where he was used to being occupied in a variety of handyman tasks such as mowing lawns and washing bodies in the hospital morgue! He had been sent to the hospital as a young boy when his constantly drunk father, who had regularly beat his mother, had died. Mother was sent to the women's wing of the psychiatric unit where she eventually died and his sister was placed in the care of Protestant nuns who ran an old folks' home. His sister is still there – as is Jean-Marie now, joining her when he retired and had left our care. He certainly was work-shy and even found peeling an orange too much trouble! But he came with pet turtle-doves and was happy to feed the family's rabbits and chickens. Of very limited intelligence he spent a lot of time dreaming of his future where he would marry and have lots of children to help him in his future bakehouse. He did actually have a 'girlfriend', much older than him and we regularly took him to meet her in the old folks' home where she was a resident and we even brought her to us for the occasional weekend.

He was certainly very different from the other man we fostered – Bernard, but they became great friends over the years they spent with us. Bernard was about the 8th child of yet another father who been reputedly constantly drunk. Of limited intelligence, in his teenage years he attended a Special School/Occupational Therapy Centre during the week, returning home for the weekends. We were able to establish that the school bus-driver had once invited Bernard to spend a weekend with him and his wife and that this became a regular occurrence, and then a permanent arrangement once Bernard left the school and the bus driver had retired.

Apparently, neither Bernard's family nor Social Services were aware of this and all went undetected until the bus-driver's wife died and her sister moved in with her brother-in-law but wanted to be rid of Bernard! This is when Social Services were contacted and we welcomed a very distressed Bernard into our home. He was truly a delight to have around, very entertaining and very biddable – albeit very wearing. His favourite activity in life was to help others – anyone, under any conditions. He had only to notice a neighbour digging a hole and he would grab the spade and finish the job... Endowed with too much initiative and an inability to foresee consequences he had to be constantly supervised and he certainly kept us on our toes for 13 years!

His one great desire was to drive a car but his spatial awareness was such that he couldn't judge the width of the road and his lack of understanding meant that, to him, triangular road signs with an 'X' on them meant there was a cemetery ahead, rather than a crossroads. He loved manipulating wood and would always haul huge loads of logs into the house. His reasoning was that there would be enough for the next few days 'but where shall we put it Bernard?'. 'Ah oui, encore une connerie!' (a self-admitted daft thing to do). One favourite 'connerie' (I think he did it on purpose to gain attention) was to bring a piece of wood into the house which was too long for the stove. 'C'est trop grand Bernard' (it's too big); 'Pas de problème Garry' and he would proceed to split it lengthways in order to make it 'smaller'...

Perhaps his most embarrassing 'connerie' was actually ordering a car! One morning, a vehicle drew-up outside our house pulling a trailer on which there was a 'voiture sans permis' which he had ordered at the local town's annual trade fair which we had all been to the previous weekend. He did present well physically and obviously he had approached the car stand without our noticing him and the car salesman had taken him to his word and was now delivering the car for Bernard to test-drive...A 'voiture sans permis' is a micro car for which one doesn't need to pass a driving test or have a licence. A very illogical situation to my mind when one realises that if one is incapable of passing the 'Code de la Route' (highway code test) or a practical driving test why should one be allowed to drive anything? These 'voitures sans permis' are very popular with drivers who lose their licences after a drink-driving offence but they are very expensive to purchase.

As Bernard wasn't actually present when the car was delivered, he didn't have the disappointment and embarrassment of coping with the situation but it was left to us to deal with the displeased salesman...

He really became an important member of the family and was loved by many of the locals. When Sue and I retired, another foster family was found for him and when we deposited him there both Sue and I had tears in our eyes – as well as Bernard. Things seemed to go well enough for him for a while; he became the husband's mate in his new family, helping in the garden and odd-jobbing outside while the wife was indoors with a mentally handicapped young woman. Then a horrific event. On the local TV news there was an item of a young handicapped woman having been murdered in her foster family and another handicapped person in the family was accused of the murder. We quickly realised that the accused person was our Bernard.

It took a lot of determined effort to establish from the Gendarmerie where Bernard was – the psychiatric hospital, to gain access to see Bernard, heavily drugged with behaviour-controlling medication – and to persuade Bernard's legal guardian, the psychiatric doctor and the 'juge d'instruction' to allow us to have Bernard back pending trial. Fortunately, the defence lawyer assigned to Bernard's case proved to be very human and supportive of Bernard and trusting towards us, accusing the authorities of illegal detention of a person against their will and demanding that he be freed. In the meantime, the autopsy revealed that the poor girl had died of a pulmonary embolism, the result of months of bad treatment, and that Bernard had not drowned her in the bath where he had been sent to fetch her for supper. Accusing one mentally handicapped person of killing another was such a convenient thing to do...

We were eventually able to woo a very shaken and mentally-damaged Bernard back to 'normality' over the next few months and to prepare him for confronting the murderer as a witness at the Tribunal. Bernard was still viewed with some suspicion, however – even by some of the people in our commune but enough people knew and trusted him to write glowing character references and Richard, our youngest son, now a web master for the 'Le Monde' newspaper group was able to persuade a journalist to come from Paris and to spend a day with us. She wrote a wonderful article about poor Bernard's experience of life and it appeared, very helpfully, on the first day of the trial (see appendix).

Poor Bernard couldn't cope with the judge dressed in his red robes and simply sobbed on the witness stand, even though I was allowed to stand next to him in support. I had tried to protect Bernard, as a registered handicapped person, saying that he would be in no fit mental state to be able to give useful testimony, but to no avail; and when I tried to insist somewhat I was informed that I could be seen as being in contempt of court ('outrage à magistrat'). The murderer got 15 years and Bernard called for champagne once we got home, shouting 'on a gagné' (we won), believing that it was all thanks to his testimony! We kept Bernard for a few more months and during that period an older brother, now retired from the army, became his legal guardian and Bernard was able to re-unite with his natural family – mother and siblings – before being placed in a wonderful family-run residential occupational centre with 5 other handicapped people where he is very happy. He some-times comes to see us, and that gives us great pleasure.

Another aspect of our life – which didn't help us to integrate but was a great help to us in the daily routine of running a smallholding – was to receive help from WWOOFERs. Originally 'Working Weekends on Organic Farms', this was an organisation through which we used to welcome individuals and couples to our small farm in Cumbria. The idea was that these people would help with daily husbandry tasks in exchange for board and lodging and a certain amount of training in organic methods of growing crops. By the time we'd arrived in France, this organisation had become known as Willing Workers on Organic Farms and had become international. Consequently, we were able to host people from all over the world for short and long periods – although, apparently the French authorities viewed this as almost 'working on the black', but we kept a low profile and called the Wwoofers 'visiting friends'. Whilst some of the volunteers were less than helpful and just looking for a cheap holiday, some proved to be a great asset to us. Bernard was particularly keen to 'teach' them how to do things! One Irish couple actually stayed for several months and were really instrumental in our being able to rebuild Le Capitaine's cottage. They brought plumbing skills and some different ways of gardening to enhance our daily lifestyle; they were a great asset to us during their stay.

One of the first jobs we had to carry out on the cottage was to install a septic tank – 'une fosse toutes eaux'. An English friend with a borrowed JCB offered to dig the hole and the trenches for the soak-away pipes but first we needed permission from the DASS ('Direction des affaires sanitaires et sociales' or Ministry of sanitation and social affairs). A phone call in July resulted in an inspector coming along. 'What's your planning permission number' – 'Haven't got one; our understanding is that don't need planning consent to renovate a house as long as you don't alter its façade', 'Where are your plans then?', 'Haven't got any, they're all in my head, We've dug the hole and the trenches, we just need you to say if they're OK', 'Draw me a thumbnail sketch then', and off he went with it. We then telephoned the nearest builders' merchants to order a tank, the necessary pipes and the limestone chippings to line the trenches with. 'Don't do limestone chippings, we sell pebbles for that job', 'well send me pebbles then', 'Can't, you're supposed to put limestone chippings in because you're in Deux-Sèvres and we're in the Charente', 'But you're our nearest merchant, only 12 kms away and the property is just 200m from the border with the Charente!', 'Can't help you'. So then we telephoned the inspector who'd been to see us just a few days before, 'He's on holiday', 'Can I speak to his assistant then', 'He hasn't got one, ring back in September' (five weeks later!) So I thought I'd check with the building planning department ('DDE'): 'Could you inform me if I'm allowed to line my trenches with pebbles please?' 'Nothing to do with us', 'But you must have a building inspector who's looked into septic tank trenches and who can tell me if I can put pebbles in them!', 'No, but you could always ask at the Mairie as they're responsible for such work in their communes now'. I thought I'd get a quicker response from the Mairie in the local town rather than the Mairie in our commune: 'Bonjour, would I be allowed to line my trenches with pebbles rather than limestone chippings please?' 'Wrong Mairie, ask at your own', 'But surely you could inform me?', 'Non', Finally 'Bonjour Claude (our new Maire) can I have your permission to line my new septic tank trenches with pebbles please? 'I've been told that such decisions are now your responsibility.' 'News to me, do what you want'! So we did but we took photos of the work once terminated, declared the job done and waited until September for the inspector to return – which he never did...

Years later we were informed that the septic tank for our main house we had had installed in accordance with current regulations in 1988 was now unacceptable. The inspector who came to visit and test the waste water system admitted that it was functioning perfectly well but as we had 4 bedrooms, a 3,500litre septic tank was considered to be too small and that we should replace it with one of 4,500litres (only about 8 000€ expense!).

'But there are only two of us now living in the house! The children have left home and as we are retired we aren't a foster family any more'. 'Well you still have 4 bedrooms and even if you don't use them your septic tank does not comply with current regulations'. 'But during the fifteen years or more when there were at least seven of us living in the house, there was never a problem with the system and your colleagues who inspected it 5 years' ago found no fault whatsoever'. 'That's not the case now, the norms have changed and I'm only doing my job in informing you...'. I've since established that at least 80 per cent of septic tanks in the area do not conform to these new regulations and whilst we are not obliged to do anything (!) if we sold the house the purchasers would have to replace the system with a larger septic tank!! I think we shall have 'problems' with French Administration until the end of our time here... Our good neighbours don't even have a septic tank – all they have is a cesspit which they have always emptied onto their fields for manure!

This little story is typical of brushes with the Administration in the French countryside but at least we were spared what must be seen as one of the worst events which happens every few years – 'le remembrement' (obligatory reparcelling of land). It had happened in our area just before our arrival and its effects were devastating. What happened was that the SAFER (Societé d'amenagement foncier et d'établissement rural) the Ministry of Agriculture's body for re-allocating land, does so in order to make small farms more viable. Farmers who have acquired new fields and bits of land over the years suddenly find that they have to part with them and receive other parcels in exchange, This supposed rationalisation of land inevitably leads to trees and hedges being cut-down and ripped-out before they are handed-over as nobody wants to give away valuable wood! The procedure can lead to very unhappy farmers and on-going resentment. It's worth noting that if you buy a field, you are not automatically entitled to the trees growing on it – they have to be negotiated separately!

We were lucky as local politicians had realised the negative aspect of so many hedges being ripped-up that a new hedge-planting scheme came into being just two years after our arrival. We were able to plant hedges with a mixed variety of trees and bushes which we were given free of charge on the perimeter of our land and 25 years later they are now full of wildlife and create a great wind-break for our beehives and our 'potager'. There is, and always has been a lot of wildlife around – to the delight of the strong hunting fraternity in the commune. The period of 'La Chasse' is from the second Sunday in September until the end of the following February. Around here, during the hunting months, it's best not to venture into the woods on Thursdays and Sundays – especially with a dog – unless you wear a bright orange jacket and make a lot of noise! Apart from deer and boar, hunted for 'la cuisine' there are also badgers, foxes, red squirrels and a host of small mammals as well as a very rich bird life. Local hunters caught, and killed, 45 foxes this year in our commune!

Unfortunately, some three years after moving here we had a new neighbour who is an ardent hunter and keeps some 16 hunting dogs which spend a lot of time barking.

There's nothing we can do about it as he keeps to the local regulations governing distances and housing conditions for his 'chiens de chasse' but one can't help feeling sorry for them locked up in their pen for so many months of the year. It's interesting to note that it was only last year that President Hollande passed a law stating that dogs and cats were actually creatures with feelings; before that, animals had no more rights than a coffee table and could be treated in any way one wished.

The hunting association in the commune organises a public banquet every year, so if one likes eating venison or boar one is not disappointed. We are not 'chasseurs' but if a deer is unfortunately involved in a traffic accident and a leg of 'chevreuil' comes our way, we do have a recipe for a wonderful wine-based marinade which makes for a memorable repast! (See recipe chapter.)

11

Pour Conclure...

In concluding this description of our attempt to become French paysans I am obliged to admit that we have actually **failed** to achieve such status! We must just admit to being seen as Country Dwellers who love living in this part of the French countryside, who make the most of our environment and who are content to know that we are genuinely held in some esteem by many of our neighbours and new compatriots – but **not** as paysans.

'Paysans', in any case, are dying out! In 1945, according to official figures, there were 10 million 'paysans' in France whereas in 1990 there were only 1 million. In 1950, there were 2 million farms and in 2010 this number had been reduced to 500,000. This gradual disappearance of the 'paysanerie' is due to the explosion of mechanisation, the ever increasing reliance on chemicals in the form of artificial fertilisers, herbicides and pesticides and the regrouping of small fields ('remembrement') to create bigger and bigger and supposedly more efficient and productive farms which need less workers; food in 'quantity rather than quality'?

Even the word 'paysan' is used less and less. These traditionally small-scale land owners who worked the land have now become 'agriculteurs' (farmers) or 'exploitants agricoles' (farmers) and are officially seen as being 'chefs d'entreprises' (Company Directors). One goat farm nearby has 450 milking goats and the 'chef d'éxploitation' gets up at 3.00am every day to get the first milking under way; not a paysan's life that I envy! Certainly, more and more children brought up on the land in France do not wish to take over from their parents in continuing the family tradition of running the farm. Instead, they become Agricultural Engineers, Advisers or Inspectors or find a career in some other aspect of research or administration in a field linked to agriculture.

Yes, we have tried very hard ever since we arrived here more than 27 years ago, to understand and adopt the ways of our French neighbours and how they make the most of their rural lives, but in the end we realise that we never had a chance! We were doomed to failure from the very start – and I think it's to do with education. In France, if you've received higher education you are seen to be of a different status than a person born to the land. French society is very hierarchical and you are required to accept your standing accordingly. It's seen through the 'vouvoiement' (addressing people as 'vous' rather than 'tu'), addressing people by 'Madame' or 'Monsieur' and behaving generally according to your station. If you act as if you're from a different layer of society – up or down, you lay yourself open to criticism.

Yes, we did apply for, and were granted French nationality. Yes, we did learn to communicate very fluently in French. Yes, we were seen by neighbours to be competent in the fields of animal husbandry and food production. Yes, we were seen to be efficient and useful in caring for handicapped fellow French citizens as a foster family. Yes, I did become a French civil servant and Sue was seen to be a good Primary school teacher. Yes, our 3 children were brought up in France, today follow careers in France and live with French partners with their French offspring and yes, we were seen to contribute fully to the social life of our rural community; but after all of these years of attempting to integrate and of trying to make a positive difference to our adopted environment we are still viewed as strangeers – people who came from elsewhere and who are not part of the 'Nous' who belong here. 'Ils ne sont pas de chez nous' (they're not from here – they're 'off-comers' as they say 'up North'). Perhaps we should have moved to a small town rather than the countryside where our presence would have been less noticed, but then we wouldn't have been trying to be 'paysans' would we?

As an ex music teacher, after a few years, I eventually missed not making music and was appointed musical director of an amateur local choir. It was made up uniquely of French singers when I was appointed and little by little, more and more British residents joined. This was particularly useful to the choir as most of these newcomers were of retirement age and had been through the British educational system when music was considered to be more important than it perhaps is today. Consequently, these people were musically literate and we were able to perform larger, more satisfying works and, working bilingually, the choir became an excellent tool for integration and Anglo-French cooperation. When I decided to retire after eight years of mostly successful and enjoyable concerts, the town's Maire awarded me a medal for services to cultural life during a memorable ceremony! What an honour! But it was still awarded to an Englishman who happened to have French nationality and not to someone seen as being a Frenchman.

Last year I was persuaded by some 'concitoyens' to put

myself up for election as Maire of our little community of 200 voters; I thought I had the right experience, useful ideas and a willingness to work hard to be able to lead a team of 10 councillors and to serve the interests of French residents and also 'European' residents (it's interesting to note, that for local elections France defines voters as either being French or European!). I obtained 23 per cent of votes but it was made clear to me by some of the older residents that while I was perhaps 'sympa' (a likeable chap), I was still an 'outsider' and I failed to be elected...

However, undeterred, Sue and I, together with some French friends in our 'commune' have since created a bilingual association of 'Bonne Entente' (goodwill and neighbourliness) to help the British residents which now make up 24 per cent of the permanent and part-time population in the village and surrounding hamlets to better integrate into the commune. We organise bi-lingual events such as banquets and concerts to remember mutual fraternisation in the trenches of Christmas 1914, 200 years of peace since Waterloo, Easter Bonnet competitions and occasions to share recipes for scones, mince pies and quiche Lorraines baked in local bread ovens and a drop of Pineau...(It's interesting to note that the membership includes more French than 'European' members...).

So if I now think back to the reasoning we had in wanting to give up all and moving to this bit of 'la France profonde'– to try our best to become French paysans, believing that they were happier than a middle-class comprehensive school Deputy Head and his family, I think that instead of becoming such, we gradually became a different breed of country folk – people who adopted many of the paysan activities and showed great understanding and sympathy for French rural ways of life and habits but we have always been and always will be 'offcomers' and held in the same light as Parisians when they move into the area!

Certainly we were never tempted to return to the UK and we have reserved our plot in the village cemetery! When our children reached the age of 16 they were given the option of renouncing their French nationality as it had been their parents' decision for them to become French when they were much younger; all three have chosen to remain French, albeit with a little exotic British 'je ne sais quoi' added to their Frenchness. They have never thought of returning to Blighty – except to show their own children the country of their birth. Our grand-children are also growing-up to be bilingual and we can pride ourselves in having contributed to the exciting adventure of the Europe of the future – as 'exotic' franco-philes who have chosen to live in France and follow the French way of life to the full.

So many of the British Expats who came to this same

area after us have ended-up returning to the UK. They came with as many different reasons for doing so as one could imagine; from older people just wanting to enjoy a quiet retirement in a part of Europe where the weather is so much kinder and there is so much less crime, to families wanting to start some sort of business enterprise, or simply to seek any sort of employment, believing it would be easy to find something they could do.Some do succeed, of course, integrate well and contribute to village life, but so many eventually return to the UK – if they can afford to, when one takes into account the difference in housing prices – disillusioned with their adventure.

Many retired people return either because they can't learn French sufficiently well, as they seem to think that mastering a foreign language can be achieved through a sort of osmosis, without working at it! and therefore find it hard to integrate – or their children don't want to come across from the UK and spend every holiday in France with them, so they miss their grandchildren – or they suddenly realise that if their spouse dies, they can't see themselves spending the last of their days in a French care home, surrounded by folk with whom they cannot communicate...

Some of the local doctors and pharmacists are to be congratulated in the way they try to deal with certain sick expat patients; others have problems to communicate. Pity the poor doctor who needs to examine a woman's breasts and asks her, in broken English, to 'Show me your tits'! having been mischievously misinformed of the correct word to use! Pity the poor English lady's embarrassment in the Chemist's shop who turns to a fellow compatriot bilingual gentleman customer and asks 'what does the chemist mean when she keeps talking about 'muguet', I thought that was a flower (Lily of the Valley) offered to ladies in France on May 1st?') and when she hears the reply 'You've got "Thrush" Madam, muguet is thrush'...

Those wanting to set-up a business also have problems trying to communicate in French and then they are faced with the not-so-small obstacle of registering their activity in France and the large obstacle of being able to satisfy French Administrative requirements when faced with less than helpful officials; Some do succeed, of course, or they fall into the trap of trying to add to the holiday rental market and renovate a second property with a view to transforming it into a 'gîte', only to find that the market is already saturated. Those looking for employment have to compete with French nationals applying for the same jobs – and a French 'patron' will never give priority over a Frenchman to a foreigner. The result is often that those who fail to find a 'proper' job with a French company will then work exclusively for other Brits – usually in the fields of renovation, gardening, caretaking, house-sitting – and often 'on the black'. If they have children of school age, often the problems of integrating into the French education system are underestimated. While some schools see having an English-speaking pupil in their classroom as a bonus, many are now tired and frustrated of constantly having to deal with unhappy children who try to speak French at school only to return home each evening where only English is spoken. British television programmes which encourage people to look across the Channel for a new home and sing the praises of moving to France have much to answer for...

These problems are only exacerbated by the size of the British community in the area. Whilst there isn't a cricket club or an English-speaking amateur dramatic club around, so many Expats follow their British ways once in France never seeking to integrate in any way, and live a life surrounded by other Expats, making little effort to understand why things might actually be done differently here. One wonders why they come and why some do stay. They just continue to live as they did in the UK, amazed that the local doctor doesn't speak English, for instance!.

They came, of course, as **'Expats'** and in no way see

themselves as 'immigrants'! The difference being, I think that Expats (or people who call themselves that) do not see themselves as being part of the new society they have chosen to live in and do not actually want to integrate. Consequently 'expat' is arguably an elitist term and many see themselves as being 'a British person living in France' rather than an 'immigrant' – someone seeking to be a living part of French Society, absorbing the French lifestyle to the full and, hopefully, adding to and enriching what is a developing multicultural society. I'm afraid I feel that many Expats actually tend to drive a wedge into the ongoing dream of 'Europeanisation' of a founder member State – and I wonder how many of them voted 'leave' in the Brexit referendum, while still wanting to live in France! Yes, we have met some!

When French neighbours and acquaintances are asked for their opinions concerning the 'invasion' of 'Europeans' over the past twenty years or so into their daily lives, they are very happy to admit that they find it as being something positive! They are in admiration for the way old ruins are transformed into wonderful homes, surrounded by colourful gardens and 'Mairies' are pleased to see more children attend schools where numbers were falling. Old village bars and cafés have been transformed into successful restaurants and the local economy does benefit from the presence of more and more new residents. These newcomers bring employment but what the French are particularly positive about is the fact that so many of the British bring 'good taste'! 'Les anglais have such good ideas for improving homes that we would never have thought of; our ideas for home improvement have evolved as a result – and so many of them are so "cool"!' 'Cool?' 'Yes, because these newcomers feel liberated from the UK administrative System, they come here with a feeling of detachment from any system and they live a freer, "cooler" life.'

Cool, maybe, but this can go in one or two ways. These Expats don't keep to traditional French meal-times and in recent years local supermarkets have started remaining open at lunch-time, which is something no shops ever did when we arrived all those years ago. They do so as so many UK residents prefer to shop at this time and have their main meal in the evening, thereby making it difficult to entertain or be entertained by French neighbours – especially when a cup of tea is asked for with most meals!

Then these are the same people who will, in any case, do most of their shopping 'on-line' from the UK and take advantage of the services of delivery companies to this region in France. I think that might be fair enough for such things as Marmite or Crumpets which are difficult to find or much more expensive in France if you can find them – and it can be quite fun introducing your French neighbours to British specialities – but what can be the point of buying cat litter, toilet paper, potatoes(!) and all of your food requirements in the UK when you're living in France? They seem to only watch satellite television programmes when watching even just the news on French television would be a great help in learning the language – although, admittedly French TV programmes are not in the same league as the BBC's!

Of course there is some resentment – the price of houses, once renovated, can then become out of the reach of some of the younger French and some preferred the old, tatty village bar as it was; old Jacques doesn't pop-in for his daily 'petit jaune' (Pastis) anymore because he feels uncomfortable in the new, plush surroundings; and Jacques's wife complains that she used to enjoy hearing nothing but the local 'patois' at market stalls, then it was also French and now it's nothing but English. 'And they've all got such big cars and the first thing they do is build a swimming pool! Ils sont bourées de fric' (they must be stuffed with money!') And then the most heinous 'faux pas' of all – mowing the lawn on a Sunday afternoon... By-laws in France are quite clear – 'No continuous sound (machines or dogs, etc) which could disturb the neighbourhood is allowed between 12.30pm and 2.00pm or after 7.00pm on a weekday and before 10.00am or after 12.00noon on a Sunday. How many times have local Maires been asked to apply the law by annoyed neighbours, and fine the miscreants ! But so many expats are 'cool' about it all; 'I don't see why I can't cut my lawn when it needs cutting, it's what I've always done...' But perhaps the greatest fault newly-arrived British people have – and certainly the one we hear most complaints about – is the way they fail to cross the street and shake the hand of (or give the 3 kisses to) a French person they know, giving just a friendly wave instead; and the way they enter a café, a restaurant or a shop and don't say a general 'Bonjour Messieurs-Dames'. Consequently, they are considered as being stand-offish or cold and unfriendly – if not downright impolite – ('il se prend pour qui celui-là?' – 'Does he think he's a superior being to us?'). It doesn't occur to the French that such people are simply demonstrating natural British 'reserve' or simply being respectful of others' privacy and not wanting to impose. Ah, 'la différence!' The 'entente cordiale is not always easy...'

12

The « Godans »

Sunday 26.06.2016 – 3 days after 'Brexit'

Today, Sue and I went to the 'foire aux pirons' (Goose Fair) in a local town; a town which counts many Expats and a town where Sue and I gave English lessons in our early days to French people who were keen to communicate with their new European neighbours via the 'Association pour la promotion des langues étrangères dans le Chef-Boutonnais'.

We bought some point-of-lay hens and a few young turkeys for Christmas and then we chatted with perplexed French locals and anxious expats. The sole topic of conversation was the British referendum of 23rd of

June and the implications of the UK leaving the European Community. Members from both the French and the British community seemed to be in a state of shock. What will really happen, what will be the consequences of such a decision for us all? Will the Brits, no longer be seen as being European, but aliens? Will they all apply for French nationality? Or will they all sell-up and go?

What to say of Victor Hugo, who in August 1849 said 'A day will come when you France, you Russia, you Italy, you England, you Germany, you all, nations of the continent, without losing your distinct qualities and your glorious individuality, will be merged closely within a superior unit and you will form the European brotherhood.'?

What to say of Winston Churchill who in September 1946 said 'If Europe were once united in the sharing of its common inheritance, there would be no limit to the happiness, to the prosperity and glory which its three or four hundred million people would enjoy. Yet it is from Europe that have sprung that series of frightful nationalistic quarrels, originated by the Teutonic nations, which we have seen even in this twentieth century and in our own lifetime, wreck the peace and mar the prospects of all mankind... there is a remedy which, if it were generally and spontaneously adopted, would as if by a miracle transform the whole scene, and would in a few years make all Europe, or the greater part of it, as free and as happy as Switzerland is today. What is this sovereign remedy? It is to re-create the European

Family, or as much of it as we can, and provide it with a structure under which it can dwell in peace, in safety and in freedom. We must build a kind of United States of Europe.' This dream was partly achieved in 1973, but now...? Now, the National Front of Marine Le Pen in France is delighted with the Brexit results and is determined to achieve the same in France with a 'Frexit'. French opinion polls concerning next year's presidential elections put Marine Le Pen in second place... But some French friends of ours, with reference to Brexit also said:

'Nous sommes très tristes et inquiets de ce résultat. We were born just after the war and our parents told us how their youth had been so marked by the terrible conflict. They often referred to it and prayed that future generations would build a better world. They placed their hope in the creation of a united Europe and shared their confidence in a better future with us.

We hold these values dearly and regret the British decision. Recently, it is true that the European dream has lost its impetus and we feel that many people have become more and more disappointed with the way the EU has developed, thereby creating a climate of fear and a tendency to become more inward-looking. People are more and more aggressive towards each other. We can only hope that this Brexit decision will encourage European leaders and leaders of all the individual member countries to work towards greater understanding and strive to make all people see the European dream in a more positive light. It's our unique opportunity to help us find our place in the world.' Our friends, then, still share the European dream as do, seemingly, the majority of local French people; we can only hope, if the Brexit decision is carried out, that we shall not see posters in the region in the near future saying: 'Cherche jeune fille croyante, de 16 ans, de nationalité française, vièrge, avec cheval et épée pour travail important'. (Wanted, a 16 year old, God-fearing French virgin girl, with horse and sword for an important job). ...and I wonder if we'll be banished or not, being called 'Godans' which is what Jeanne d'Arc shouted at the English during the siege of Orléans...(People damned by God). However, at our village fête this week to mark 'Bastille Day', whole pigs were roasted over glowing embers and I happened to mention to a few of the French gathered around the fire during the apéritif 'Perhaps you'd like to throw "les anglais présents à la fête onto the fire at the end of the cooking, to avenge Joan of Arc and "le Brexit?"' 'Non, non' they all cried out, 'On vous aime trop; le fait que vous avez brulé Jeanne d'Arc sur le bûcher c'est du passé! Maintenant, vous êtes nos amis et il y aurait beaucoup moins de monde à notre fête aujourd-hui si vous n'étiez pas là!' (We like you too much; the fact that you burned

Joan of Arc is past history! Now, you are our friends and if you weren't here today there would be less people to enjoy the day's festivities.)

PART TWO

13

« A la soupe! »
(Come and Eat!)

In our attempt to become 'paysans', our life, from the very beginning, was punctuated by the rhythm of the seasons and the growing cycle – and the way daily life was and is divided up by mealtimes. We did not, however, follow all of the traditions observed by locals in times gone by to the extent that only the man of the house – « le patron » – (and his labourers, if he had any) and his children sat at table to eat. « La patronne » – the lady of the house – would eat, standing or seated, by the fire where she had prepared the meal which she was now about to serve at the table, keeping an eye on both the « marmite » (cooking pot) and the fire.

In the past, in these parts, during the winter months, the main diet centred around dried white beans, peas, lentils or potatoes, accompanied by some sauce or other which had simmered on the fire all morning. Any meat or fish on offer was mere accompaniment to this starchy base, and not vice versa, as today. Fat for cooking came mostly from the pig, geese or ducks, with butter when it was available, and walnut oil being mostly used for dressing salads; the walnuts having been collected locally, shelled during the winter months around the fireside with everyone lending a hand, and taken to the local nut press (two kilos of kernels would yield one litre of oil)

In the warmer months « on vivait sur le jardin » (the garden provided most of the food) – peas, green beans, brassicas, salads, etc. as well as soft and hard fruits. To this could be added all that could be found growing in the hedgerows, field and forest – from dandelion leaves to various mushrooms, walnuts, chestnuts, snails, wild birds and honey (honey production is very important around here).

Soup was so important that the word « soupe » was used to refer to the main meal itself. « A la soupe » was the call to table. Lucienne, our neighbour, born in the village, says that when she was young « we had soup for every meal, every day, Winter and Summer » – water, bread and vegetables. « The best soups were the thickest, in which the spoon would stand upright »!

There must be as many recipes for soup as there are grandmothers! Here are a few genuine, traditional recipes of « paysanne soupe » which you won't want to try...

1. Soupe de Vie (Soup for Staying Alive)
12 peeled garlic cloves, a bunch of thyme, rosemary and bay leaves, 1 litre of boiling water, 3 tablespoons of oil or melted fat, salt to taste.

Boil for 15 minutes and pour onto dry bread in a soup dish.

2. Soupe à la grolle (Blackbird or Crow soup)
Pluck and draw the bird; cut off the legs. Brown all over in fat or butter. Add chopped carrots, turnips, celeriac and cover with water. Bring to the boil and then simmer for one hour. Add a sliced cabbage. After 30 minutes of further simmering add 4 sliced potatoes and boil further. Bon appétit!

3. Soupe à l'oseille (Sorrel soup)
2 bunches of sorrel, chopped and fried in butter or pig

fat. After 15 mins add 1½ litres of hot water and season with salt and pepper. Add 5 or 6 sliced potatoes and boil for 30 mins. Serve, if possible, with a beaten egg for greater richness.

4. La mitonnée (A 'Simmering')
Left-over pieces of dry bread covered with water. Add a pinch of salt and a bunch of chives. Boil for 45 mins. Once the soup is really thick, remove the chives and add a little red wine.

Traditional soup recipes of a more acceptable nature for today's palate include:

1. Soupe 'Marie-Jeanne'
4 broccolli heads, 800 gms of « petit salé » (salted pork belly), 4 potatoes, 80gms butter, 4 garlic cloves, slices of dry bread.

Boil the piece of salted pork with the broccolli for 1 ½ hours. Add the potatoes and the garlic and cook for a further 20 mins. Remove the broccolli and crush with a fork. Add a knob of butter to each portion of broccolli placed on individual plates. Surround each serving with pieces of potato. Cube the cooked meat and place a portion on each plate. Place slices of bread into individual soup dishes and pour on the liquid. Each person eats from both dishes – soup and bread/broccolli, meat and potato.

2. Pot au feu (Pot on the Fire)

A hearty, meat-based soup still very popular today, appearing at village feasts, and a meal often eaten by many families in the Winter months. Ideally, a selection of cuts of beef are used – rump or topside, rib and chuck which are strung together. The meat is browned in whatever fat is available and to this are added leeks, carrots, turnip and an onion pricked with cloves with a bouquet garni of thyme, parsley and bay leaves. Cover with cold water (6 litres for every 1 kg) and add a handful of coarse salt. Boil and skim off the rising scum regularly; then simmer for 4 hours at least. Add chunks of green cabbage after 2 hours – and some potatoes if you wish. Remove and set aside the meat and vegetables and re-boil the liquid with a handful of vermicelli.

The soup is served first, followed by the meat and vegetables accompanied by Dijon mustard and chunks of bread. A very filling meal, giving one a 'comfortable feeling'!

3. Soupe de moules au vin blanc

Mussels from the coastal town of Marennes – which is also well-known for its oyster beds – are the « bouchot » variety; they are reared on ropes suspended in the sea and are relatively small, but quite delicious and a very popular food. They can be cooked in a very large pan or in specially-designed individual pans from which each person will eat his or her portion, using the lid for the discarded empty shells.

For each portion of mussels (600g per person if its for a main meal) you will need butter, an onion, a carrot, a small leek and a piece of celery to which are added thyme, bay leaves, parsley, white wine, water, salt and pepper.

Place the mussels in cold water and reject any which have opened. Clean-off bits of rope and barnacles. Brown the chopped onion in 30g melted butter, add the seasoning, vegetables and herbs and fry for a couple of minutes. Pour on 2 glasses of dry white wine and some water. Allow to simmer. Once the carrot is cooked pour-in the mussels and put the lid on. A few minutes are all that is needed for the mussels to cook. Once the mussels have opened serve immediately, rejecting any mussels which have remained tight shut.

14

Special Local
Traditional Dishes

1. Farci poitevin

This speciality is only found in the relatively small area
south of Poitiers and north of Confolens. « Un plat qui
ne coute rien, que du temps; c'est une maison à bâtir » (A
dish which costs nothing to prepare other than the time
it takes; it's like building a house) It's served-up during
the period from April to June, when the green ingredients are tender. A royal, green-domed and imposing dish
when laid steaming on the table. You will need a dozen
large cabbage leaves, with the thicker stems whittled-
down somewhat. These are then boiled to soften and

then cooled. The next stage is the one which takes time and a lot of patience; you need to cut very finely, with a knife or preferably a pair of scissors, the following: 8 bunches of sorrel, 4 handfuls of cabbage (without the stems), 4 lettuces, a few stems of chard (or the white part of 2 leeks), 1 large onion, a bunch of parsley and a bunch of chives.

The first time I attempted the dish I was reprimanded by our neighbour Lucienne as she considered I hadn't cut the ingredients finely enough – and I had to start again. It was also the occasion when I had to beg parsley from her as mine hadn't germinated. She did give me some but then laughed and laughed, saying that if parsley didn't grow « chez quelqu'un » he wasn't in love and he wasn't the boss in his own home– but his wife was! The mixture is then stirred together to which 750 grams of very fatty salted pork have been added, together with a handful of fresh breadcrumbs, a large pinch of flour, salt, pepper, grated nutmeg and at least 6 beaten eggs. This is then wrapped in the parboiled cabbage leaves and then into a damp teatowel and the whole ball is then placed in a special farci net (rather like a string shopping bag) or tied-up with string to keep it together, before being placed in a large pan containing enough water (or stock made from a marrow bone) to cover the contents and to which are added thyme and bay leaves. Allow to simmer for at least 3 hours. This is a poor man's dish and the ingredients can vary from one village to another – the addition of turnip, swede, carrots, spinach or potatoes, for instance. It can be served warm (when it is at its best) or cold – as a complete meal or as an accompaniment to pork, lamb or goat meat. It can also be sliced when cold and fried (with an egg?). I suppose it's a sort of 'bubble and squeak'.

2. Chevreau à l'ail vert (Kid with Green Garlic)

Prepared only in the Spring, when the garlic in the potager has fine green shoots and the young kid has been weaned from its mother; An annual traditional dish.

Take a kid, cut into pieces (or a whole leg) and gently fry in fatty cubes of salted pork- « lardons » (bacon pieces) and a knob of butter. Add salt, pepper and a handful of chopped garlic shoots. If you're not a gardener, you could pick wild garlic (« ail des ours ») in the forest but the flavour is less strong. When browned all over add a glass and a half of water and two soup spoons of eau de vie and 4 or 5 sliced carrots. Some cooks also add a veal trotter, cut into pieces. Simmer for 4 hours or for the leg, roast in the oven as you would for a leg of lamb.

3. Gibelotte de lapin (Sautéed Rabbit)

Cut a rabbit into 6 pieces (4 leg joints and 2 from the

back) and roll in flour. Brown in melted butter in a large, heavy pan with a few lardons (cubes of bacon), chopped shallots, garlic cloves, chopped parsley and thyme and a pinch or two of allspice. Cover the meat with red wine which must be boiled in order to burn off the alcohol content with a lighted match and simmer very slowly until the meat falls off the bone. Half way through the cooking you may wish to add baby mushrooms or dried, stoneless prunes; you may also wish to stir-in the rabbit's blood, which you set aside when you killed the rabbit, to enrich the sauce; you may also wish to thicken your sauce by adding slices of « pain d'épices » (a spicy bread with honey) before serving. « Un vrai délice » (truly delicious). In the North of France, brown ale replaces the wine...

4. Canard farci (Stuffed Duck)

Soak the duck liver and heart in cold water. Powder the inside of the carcass with salt, pepper and powdered marjoram.

Chop the heart and liver and mix in a little flour with salt and pepper and gently fry in a little butter. Take 500gms of cooking apples, peel and chop.

Mix in a bowl, the apples, a chopped onion, 2 slices of fresh bread, cubed, 100g of salt dried ham (jambon sec de campagne), the heart and liver mixture and stir-in an egg beaten in 2 tbs of milk.

Force this stuffing into the bird and sew-up.

Place the duck, breast down, in a buttered oven dish into which is a layer of water just covering the bottom.

Place in the oven at 200°c.

After 15 mins turn the bird over and add 40g of butter.

Baste the duck regularly for an hour and then place 2 sliced eating apples around the duck and sprinkle with a little sugar. Cook for a further 15mins. We've often eaten this at Paul and Lucienne's and it really is delicious.

5. Civet de chevreuil (Venison Casserole)

Roe deer are numerous in this area and one has to be careful driving as they can rush out of a copse, unexpectedly, and run into you, causing considerable damage to your car. Venison is readily available from a hunter – or it is possible to acquire a leg joint as a result of a road accident...

To make a truly wonderful marinade and sauce to accompany you need 3 tbs oil, 2 large chopped onions, 2 sliced, medium carrots, a chopped bunch of parsely, a bay leaf and some thyme as well as 3 cloves of garlic, 2 shallots, 6 black pepper corns and salt. Fry and simmer together the above ingredients and add 1 glass of wine vinegar and 1 glass of water. Simmer for 30 mins and allow to cool. Once cooled, place the pieces to be casseroled or the leg to be roasted into this marinade, adding sufficient wine to cover the meat. Leave to rest overnight.

Cover and place in the oven at 200°c. After 1 hour add 250g of mushrooms and cook further until the meat is tender. If the sauce seems to be too 'thin', continue cooking without the lid on. Best served with small, boiled potatoes.

6. Mouclade (Mussels in a creamy sauce)

For 1kg mussels (moules de bouchot) you will need 25g butter, 30g fresh cream, 10g flour, 10cl white wine or pineau, the juice of ½ lemon, 1 clove of garlic, 5g of curry powder, 1 egg yolk, salt, pepper and chopped parsley.

Throw the mussels into boiling water (having cleaned and sorted them first) until they open. Drain, keeping the water aside. Empty every other mussel shell.

Melt the butter and stir in the flour, strain and add the water to make a sauce. Add the mussels (shelled and unshelled), salt, pepper and simmer for 5–7 mins.

Away from the pan, mix together the lemon juice, cream, egg yolk and curry powder. Add to the mussels and cook for 5 mins.

Serve with chopped parsley. Instead of using cutlery you can use an empty mussel bivalve as a pair of pincers to winkle out the remaining mussels from their shells – licking the shells before disposing of them! Delicious!

7. Anguilles au vin (Eels in Wine)

The town of Niort – our County Town – lies on the edge of marshland – Le Marais Poitevin, which is a popular tourist attraction. In the network of canals, eels are caught in basket traps. Considered a local delicacy, there are several ways of serving them. This recipe is popular:

For a good-sized eel, skinned, gutted and washed you will need a bottle of red wine, a chopped onion, parsley, bay leaves, garlic, thyme, salt, pepper and carrots.

Cut the eel into chunks. Pour the wine into a casserole, add chopped onions, sliced carrots, the garlic cloves, herbs and seasoning Boil this court bouillon for an hour. Add the pieces of eel and cook for 15 mins. The dish is ready for serving but even better is to make a sauce:

Melt 50g butter and add 20 small white onions and 250g of button mushrooms; season and mix well. Filter the court bouillon and add two glassfulls to the sauce mixture. Serve the pieces of eel with this sauce accompanied by fried croutons.

8. Brandade de morue (Salt Cod Pie)

A very popular poor-man's dish, this, but full of essential ingredients for a healthy body – nitrogen, phosphorous, calcium and a variety of vitamins. Salted cod has been sold at markets in France since the 15th century.

For 800g of salted cod you will need 800g of potatoes, a whole head of garlic, 2 onions, 2tbs of oil and pepper.

Desalt the fish in cold water for 24 hours, changing the water several times. Skin the fish. Boil the potatoes (without salt) and poach the fish twice, changing the water.

Flake the fish and remove the bones carefully.

Fry the chopped onions and the garlic in oil, then add the fish. Drain and mash the potatoes. Add the fish to the mash and onion mixture. Place in a large dish or in individual ramekins and bake in an oven at 150°c until the top is browned. Serve with a dressed, green salad.

Some cooks add fresh cream or milk to the mashed potatoes.

9. Les « Mohjettes » (White Beans)

These beans make for a complete meal. They grow well in this area and once dried can be kept for months. They were certainly an important part of « paysan » meals in bygone years, served with a sauce; but today they are often served with a meat dish too. Further to the South they are certainly an essential ingredient in « Cassoulet ».

Before cooking, they should be soaked overnight in cold water with a bunch of sage; the sage reduces the amount of flatulence these beans can provoke to the digestion...

To prepare the dish, fry a chopped onion in butter or pig fat or duck/goose fat or even oil. Add a sliced carrot, a piece of celery, a quartered tomato, sage and other herbs of your choice, along with salt and pepper – and perhaps a couple of mushroom halves or a sweet pepper – anything to add flavour to the beans. When softened, add the drained beans and a glass of white wine. Cover the whole with water and simmer for several hours, topping-up the water as necessary.

They really are good enough to eat as a dish in themselves but they also accompany sausage, a gammon steak or a pork chop admirably well. The Cassoulet dish consists of these beans with a piece of cured duck, a piece of salted pork and a thick Toulouse sausage.

10. Confit (d'Oie ou de Canard) (Goose or Duck Conserve)

2 breasts and 2 thighs per bird! – the carcasses can be used in another recipe...

Truly wonderful food, this – and duck or goose fat is healthy fat!

Trim the pieces of meat, removing any ragged bits of skin and cutting off all of the excess fat. You may decide to cut the goose breasts into two if they are too big for one individual portion. Roll the joints in coarse sea salt and add pepper and a pinch of allspice or just cinnamon as well as several bay leaves. Place in an earthenware crock for at least a day and a half.

After the meat has rested, dissolve enough goose fat as is necessary to line the bottom of a heavy pan and carefully add a glass of water and then place each piece of meat with the skin side downwards to melt into the liquid, having brushed off any excess salt. Some people add garlic cloves.

The heat must be very low indeed. Allow the joints to cook for at least 3 hours – all day is better! Remember to turn the meat frequently, ensuring that it is just gently bubbling and not frying. The smell arising from the pan is quite heavenly and the meat is ready when it just falls off the bone. Drain the joints and fry parboiled potatoes in the fat to serve with the meat with a sprinkling of parsley. That's all you need for an excellent meal but you could also serve it with green peas or a dressed, green salad.

When you're cooking the joints you could also add the gizzards which you will also have conserved in the salt and spice mixture. These, cut up small are delicious on a green salad with walnuts or cubes of goats' cheese – especially the yellow-hearted frisée variety or rocket. (salade aux gésiers).

The necks can also be conserved – there is more meat on them than you might think – and cooked with the joints, the neck skin can be used as a sort of sausage which can be stuffed with the deboned meat mixed with chopped shallots and herbs...

The carcasses can simply be placed close to a roaring fire to roast. Scraped clean they make for a tasty snack. Alternatively, chop the carcass into manageable pieces and place into a heavy pan with chopped onion a little flour, chopped chives, thyme, bay, lemon zest, pepper and salt to which red wine and a little water is added. Simmer for a good hour and then remove the pieces and scrape. To the meat which you return to the sauce you can add the chopped liver. Delicious spread on toasted bread!

11. « Tomates farcies » (Stuffed Tomatoes)

Everyone around here grows large tomatoes for stuffing. The favourite variety is called « St Pierre » but there are lots of other varieties available now. The best way to cook them is in one of the many surviving bread ovens still to be found in most of the villages around. There is even a « Fête de la Tomate » in our commune every September which attracts over a hundred « convives » who come from near and far just to eat a stuffed tomato and take part in country dancing or a game of « boules /pétanque ».

Today, many people go for the ready-made « farce » (forcemeat) sold in the supermarkets but, obviously, it's best to make your own stuffing, free from preservatives.

You need to slice the top – or the bottom – off each tomato and empty it out carefully with a spoon. It might seem logical to cut the top off, but then, once the tomato is stuffed and the lid put on again, the calix is in prime position! Better to cut a slice off the bottom of the tomato and once this slice is replaced after stuffing, you have an attractive, domed top when you place the tomato upside down!

Once emptied, the tomatoes should be placed upside down to drain. For the « farce »(stuffing) I have always used 2/3 pork mince with 1/3 veal mince. Well seasoned with thyme, parsley, salt and pepper, beaten eggs are added together with a small quantity of the chopped tomato flesh (you can use the rest in sauces or a soup).

Then you have to choose to follow either the most popular way – that of putting the raw stuffing into the tomato before cooking or of cooking the stuffing thoroughly before putting it in the raw tomato, freezing and finish cooking at a later date (this way the tomatoes keep their shape).

If you're going to cook them straight away, place them side by side in an oven dish into which you have poured uncooked rice, salt, pepper and a little oil. You need to fill the dish as otherwise the tomatoes will collapse during cooking. Cover with foil. Once the meat is cooked, remove the foil to allow the tomatoes to brown a little.

If you're using a local bread oven, the cooking time will depend on where you placed your dish – it's obviously warmer in the middle of the oven than at the edge. Juice will have come out of the tomatoes during cooking and will have allowed the rice to cook. Obviously, if the rice has dried-out somewhat, you can add some of the chopped tomato flesh you have left over.

12. « Cagouilles/Sauce aux lumas » (Snails)

Two sorts of snails are collected from roadsides around here after rain – the « escargot de bourgogne » (Helix poatia) and the « petit gris » (Crytomphalus aspersus). The latter may be collected at any time of the year but the larger Burgundy variety only during the period from 1st July to 31st March. It is illegal to collect or to sell them in April, May and June as this is the period of reproduction.

Only specimens which measure at least 3cm in diameter are permitted to be collected whereas any sized « petit gris » is fair game so long as the opening to the shell has developed a hard edge. As for collecting forbidden varieties of shellfish on the coast at certain times of the year, Gendarmes could be patrolling and will fine people not keeping to the law!

Personally, I love snails stuffed with butter and parsley and cooked in the oven – especially with a glass of champagne! (in the past, people would simply put them close

to the fire in the kitchen, winkle-out the rubbery mol-
luscs and eat them with a little salt) but in this area of
France the traditional way is to eat them in a stew/sauce.

For 4 people you will need 80 snails which have been
starved in a metal net or basket for a few days so that their
systems will have cleared through. They are then placed
in a coarse salt and vinegar mixture which makes them
disgorge all of their slime (yes, it doesn't sound appetising and it doesn't look appetising either. However, once
rinsed in cold water they look better...

Prepare a « court bouillon » by adding a large, finely
chopped onion and 2 sliced carrots to a large pan half-
filled with cold water which contains a bouquet garni, a
clove, salt and pepper. Once boiling, add the snails and
cook on a high heat for 1 hour, skimming off the rising
scum as necessary.

Now chop 4 shallots and 4 garlic cloves and soften
them in melted butter with a handful of lardons (cubes
of fatty bacon). Pour on a bottle of red wine, bring to
the boil and burn-off the alcohol with a lighted match.
Add the snails, court-bouillon and a spoonful of flour.
Simmer for an hour. Not at all my 'cup of tea' but the dish
is popular at « sauce aux lumas soirées » in the Autumn
months where villagers will gather together in the village
hall and crack walnuts together, eat a bit of farci, a piece
of goat's cheese and a dessert accompanied by « vin

nouveau ». « Une veillée », these evenings are called – very useful for catching-up on local gossip!

13. Poule au pot (Chicken in a Stewpot)

A real classic dish this, not just from these parts but from the whole of France. The recipe supposedly goes back to the late 16th Century when the then king of France, Henri IV is reputed to have said « Je veux que chaque laboureur de mon royaume puisse mettre la poule au pot le dimanche » (I want every ploughman/labourer in my kingdom be able to have a chicken cooked in a stewpot every Sunday).

This, of course, does not refer to a young pullet or a young cock you might have fattened-up; it refers to an old hen which is past laying or an old cock (« coq au vin ») which doesn't do his 'stuff' anymore with his harem.

Dispatch the bird with a clout on the head with a heavy stick and then slit it's throat, being careful to collect every drop of blood. The blood will be used to enrich your sauce – or you could fry it and eat with a fried egg; « Sangatte », this is called. Some of the locals would then cut off the coxcomb for use in pâtés.

Once plucked, singed, drawn and thoroughly cleaned in and out – if you're squeamish you might want to cut off the feet and the head but, traditionally, they are part of the dish.

Place the bird in a very large pan (there will be lots of other ingredients) and cover with water and bring to the boil; once it boils, skim off the rising scum. In the meantime prepare the following: 1 chopped onion, 2 sliced leeks, 1 or 2 celery stalks and add this to the stock with salt, pepper and a bouquet garni of thyme, parsley and bay leaves once there is no further scum.

Cut-up a green cabbage into 4 or more pieces, removing the thick stalk and add to the stock after half an hour of boiling. Put a lid on and continue to cook for a further 30mins. Now add 1 large carrot per person invited to eat, turnip, some swede and any other vegetable which takes your fancy – parsnip, for instance? Continue cooking for another 30mins. Taste the stock to check on seasoning and adjust as necessary. Add a large potato per person – whole or cut into large pieces. Cook for at least 30 mins more.

Once the potatoes are cooked you can see if the bird falls into pieces easily; if not cook further. Joint the bird and place a piece on a pile of vegetables (try and make sure each person has a piece of each vegetable) on individual plates. You can serve the stock as a soup for a starter if you wish – don't forget to do the « godaille » (degreasing your plate with a drop of red wine) – before going on to the meat and vegetables. Alternatively, you could use the stock to make a good risotto.

This recipe is not quite like the « Coq au vin » for which you would add a bottle of red wine to half the amount of water at the beginning of cooking. You would then not drink the stock as a soup but boil it down somewhat before thickening with the blood and with a little flour and serve as a sauce.

15

« Le Cochon » (The Pig)

Whole books have been written about « la cuisine du cochon » (dealing with the pig in the kitchen) featuring hundreds of recipes One pig could never provide enough meat to satisfy the sheer variety of possibilites and so, choices have to be made on how to make the best of the pig the family has fattened over a few months.

For the « paysan », the pig was the 'king of the far-myard' when it came to providing meals, with poultry and rabbits following behind. Piggy costs little to rear; he eats anything and everything including your hand if you leave it long enough in front of his snout, to greasy dishwater and « dans le cochon, tout se mange sauf son cri » (everything in a pig can be eaten – except its squeal). The only tiny bit you can't actually eat is the gallbladder – and this was used for facilitating the removal of splinters once it had been dried in the hearth.

1. Boudin noirs (Blackpudding)

Immediately after killing piggy, his blood is collected and vigorously stirred to which is added a splash of vinegar to stop it clotting. To this will later be added piggy's cheeks and perhaps a bit of the bloody throat, cut while he is still hanging and before being eviscerated. Traditionally, the men clean piggy out while the women make the black-puddings in the kitchen.

The cheeks are cut into long strips and simmered in hot water before being fed through the meat mincer. This is then added to the blood, which may have needed filtering if it hadn't been stirred correctly and contains clots. Six finely chopped onions are added together with a large bunch of chopped parsley, salt, pepper and a mixture of powdered spices (we use a commercial mixture called « Rabelais ») – cinnamon, ginger, cloves, nutmeg, etc.

The whole of this is then put through the mincer with a sausage funnel attached into the sausage skin (a long skin which is tied up every few centimetres, according to the length of sausage you desire). Sausage skins are readily available in our local supermarkets and quite

honestly it is so much easier to use these industrially produced varieties rather than making your own, regardless
of how self-sufficient you wish to be as the process
is not a pleasant job and the risks of food poisoning
considerable!

If you are really determined, however, here's how to
proceed: the intestines, freshly removed from Piggy, and
therefore still warm, must be carefully washed in lots of
warm and then cold water – before they have time to start
fermenting! They then need to be scraped clean of any
bits of 'meat' and placed in a solution of vinegar and cold
water (30–50g vinegar to every 1 lt of water.) in regular,
manageable lengths. Then you must blow into them to
ensure there are no splits or holes. They are then ready
for use but they can be stored in brine or in coarse salt in
a pottery jar – or frozen for later use.

The black sausages are then placed in hot – but NOT
boiling water, as they will split – and simmered for up to
30 minutes or so. They are ready to eat once blood does
not appear on the skin when the sausage is pricked with
a needle. Once cooled they can be put into the freezer.
Different from British black puddings as they don't
contain large pieces of fat, they are delicious and usually
fried with mashed potato (purée de pommes de terre).

Once the puddings are removed from the pan, the
remaining liquid becomes the basis of a soup...

2. Andouillette (Chitterling Sausage)

This has to be mentioned as it's a very popular local delicacy, but I hate it! To me, it has a clingy odour when cooked which is very reminiscent of when you empty Piggy of his innerds – the smell which seems to stick to your hands for days after piggy-killing day.

Fresh intestines and chitterlings, pepper, wine, onion and seasonings are the main ingredients and once cooked, the sausage-shaped 'delicacies' are eaten hot or cold.

The various intestines of different calibers, once thoroughly cleaned-out, are soaked in brine for half a day – brine with mixed spices, grey pepper powder and dried savoury. The drained intestines are then cut to the same length – about 60cms.

The thinnest dimension intestine is then nailed to a board at the end of a table and the next, slighly larger intestine is slipped over the first, like a sock; then a third, and a fourth until the ensemble makes a large concentric cylinder of skins. A mixture of salt, pepper and spices can be powdered between each layer and the large intestine is then tied at either end.

This is then usually smoked. (A smoker can be easily made with a bit of imagination from an old, domestic refrigerator which has been stripped of its insulation so that you are left with an empty metallic shell. Cut a hole into the top and fix a metal plate a third of the way up. Onto this shelf you put oak or beech sawdust which is then heated to smoking point by a gas ring placed below the shelf.)

After smoking for a few hours the andouillette is then tightly wrapped in a tea-towel and allowed to simmer in a stock made from water with bay leaves, thyme and carrots for 90 minutes. Suspend from a nail and allow to cool. One restaurant, not 5 kms from us, specialises in serving this delicacy which is home-made from their black saddleback pigs. We don't eat there...

3. «Fressure » (Pluck Stew)
Another very local, and to my mind, even more unappetising dish... It consists of mincing meat from the head and throat together with skin, lungs, pancreas, onions, bread, salt, pepper and seasoning with any left-over blood. This mixture is boiled for half a day and served with mohjettes...

4. « Pieds de cochon » (Trotters)
This is reputed to be the favourite dish of a local politician, Prime Minister for a time, a few years ago. Split each trotter into two and place in a heavy pan with thyme, bay leaves, carrots, an onion spiked with cloves, parsley, chives and half a bottle of white wine. Simmer on a very

low heat for 24 hours, checking regularly on the level of the liquid, adding wine and/or water, as necessary.

Allow to cool and rest for a further 24 hours and a short time before serving fry sweet peppers in butter and place the trotters into the mixture, stirring well. Then roll the trotters in fresh breadcrumbs before grilling and serving with a glass of white wine – a local wine such as 'Haut Poitou' or a vin Charentais.

5. « Oreilles de cochon » (Pig's Ears.)

« Dans le cochon, tout est bon » (Everything is good to eat in a pig) and the ears are reputedly a real treat. They contain little fat and are crunchy...

They must first be boiled in a stock made from a leek, carrots, an onion pricked with cloves, various herbs and water. Boil the ears in this for 3 hours, then drain and cool.

Dust the ears with flour, dip them in beaten egg and then cover them with dry breadcrumbs (you can make your own by putting slices of bread into the oven and when they are browned you can crush them with a rolling pin in a paper bag). Then fry for 5 minutes in oil or butter and serve with a green salad. Crunchy!

You can do more or less the same thing with Piggy's tail, if you haven't put it in a blackpudding as a joke for someone!

6. « Jambon Sec de pays » (Dry, Salt-cured Ham)

Not uniquely local this recipe, nor even uniquely French, but here's how it's done here:

1. Choose which back leg you wish to use. Thérèse, one of our older neighbours who always insisted on our help at pig-killing time was adamant that you should only use the leg which had been uppermost when Piggy fell after having been stunned – less risk of bruising, she said.

2. Cut off the trotter (see previous recipe).

3. Decide whether to debone or not. If boned, there is less risk of failure in the curing process if the weather is warm as it can be difficult to push enough salt into the flesh around the bone, and this is where the meat could start to smell and rot. Piggy should only be killed in a month with an 'r' in it.

4. Place the leg on a sloping board, with the large part facing down the incline and allow to drain for 2 days in a cool place – in a meat safe is best, away from flies.

5. Cover with coarse sea salt and 50g of potassium nitrate. Ensure that you cut around the knuckle end of the bone, if you haven't deboned, and force in a lot of salt. Leave on the board for 10–12 days, turning every day.

6. Wipe clean with vinegar and eau de vie.

7. Make a cold sauce with ½ litre of vinegar and ½ litre of eau de vie, 50g pepper, parsley, chives, chervil, bayleaves,

thyme and spices; rub this around the whole of the leg which you then place in a plastic or pottery dish (not metallic). Turn and pour on the sauce every day until the liquid disappears.

8. Hang the ham in a flyproof muslin bag (« sac à jambon »!) in a cool place – « garde à manger » to completely dry. If you deboned the joint, it's best to place it in a tight net or to truss it up first so that it will retain a good shape while drying.

9. It is eaten (without cooking) in very fine slices – paper thin – delicious with half a Charentais melon containing a drop of pineau – a classic starter for any Summer meal.

7. Viande de porc en saumur (Pork in Brine)
Make a sweet brine from 10kg of coarse sea salt dissolved in 10 litres of hot water and 1kg of sugar. Add 15 litres of cold water, a sliced onion and herbs and spices.

When cold, add whatever cuts of meat you wish and leave for 10 days in a cool place. This is the way to make those ever-so-useful « lardons » which appear in so many recipes, from « poule au pot » to « mohjettes » and, whilst it isn't a local dish but all the same very popular, « choucroûte » requires meat from your « saumur » as well as a variety of sausages. The cuts can then be smoked in your (fridge) smoker if desired.

8. Rillettes, Grillons, Pâtés et Terrines

Which to choose? *Grillons*, the coarser version of the four, is the most basic pork dish which is traditionally eaten at any meal. Paul, our neighbour, eats it every day on bread for breakfast with a drop of red wine. It used to be preserved in earthenware pots covered by a layer of molten pig fat and the pot covered with muslin or grease-proof paper and tied with rafia. Today, grillons are more likely to be ' sterilised ' in Kilner-type jars (« bocaux à stériliser »).

To make grillons, take 4cm cubes of meat and fat taken from the breast and the shoulder and add any unwanted bits from trimming joins and chops, etc. Place this in a large pan with 1tbs of salt per kilo of meat, 1tsp pepper per kilo, no spices or herbs or onions – just « nature ». Once the meat starts to simmer on a low heat, bones may be added (if you're not making chops, but steaks or roasts for instance, you will have ribs which you can add). Stir regularly to prevent the meat sticking to the bottom of the pan. Several hours of slow cooking are necessary to produce good grillons, the excess fat being poured-off and kept in jars in a cool place for later use. They are then allowed to cool, the bones are removed and the grillons are often eaten with a pickled gherkin or two – but not pickled onions or chutney or piccallili which do not appear on the table in these parts.

Rillettes contain at least 40 % fat whereas grillons about 25 %. Small pieces of very fatty pork meat are placed in a heavy pan over a gentle heat with a little salted water and stirred repeatedly until the water has evaporated completely. Nothing else is added. The cooked meat is then crushed with a fork into the molten fat to which more salt, pepper and spices may be added. Stored in jars with a layer of fat at the top. Eaten cold, rillettes are spread on crusty bread as a snack or a starter, or on a hot jacket potato as a meal with a green salad.

Pâté is minced pork and fat (less fat than for rillettes) to which has been added some liver, salt, pepper and 2 eggs for every kilo of meat with a splash of eau de vie or cognac and a pinch of nutmeg. Today this raw mixture is placed into sterilising jars topped with a bayleaf, securely fastened and then boiled for 2¼ hours. The jars are then allowed to cool in the water, checked to make sure they have sealed correctly and then stored.

Terrines To every kilo of lean meat add 600g of fatty meat, 1 onion, 2 garlic cloves, a large bunch of parsley, thyme, rosemary and bay leaves together with a pinch of nutmeg, powdered cloves, 4g pepper, 15g salt and 1 egg with ½ glass of cognac. You may also add some pig's liver or poultry/rabbit livers if you wish. This mixture is then finely minced and placed in an earthenware/pottery terrine dish and covered with the « crépinette » (the caul or thin net membrane which covers the intestines) or with fine slices of smoked or unsmoked ham or bacon. The terrine is then placed in the oven in a bain-marie. Cook in the oven at 180°c for 2 hours, remembering to top-up the water in the bain-marie as necessary.

9. Other Piggy Dishes

These include « Fromage de Tête » (Brawn), « Pâté de Pâques » or « Pâté en Croûte » (Pork pie), « Langue » (Tongue), soaked in brine for 2 days, cooked and then peeled before eating, « Saucisson » (Salami-type cured sausages), sausages, roasts, steaks and casseroles, but none of these are any more typical of the area than for other parts of France.

16

« C'est gratuit! »
(Free Food Recipes)

1. Gâteau de châtaignes (Chestnut Cake)

This area is fabulous for chestnuts. Some of the trees are hundreds of years old and have surprising shapes. Their fruit used to be an essential part of the local economy – as flour, as an accompaniment to various meats (especially as a stuffing for poultry and as an accompanying vegetable with roast pork), with fish (monkfish terrine or stuffed salmon), as a starter (in a soufflé or roasted and added to « salade aux gésiers » or goat's cheese salad) and as a dessert (flans, charlottes and various cakes) as well as marron glâcé...honey from chestnut blossom is dark and rich. Of course, they can just be grilled on a barbecue and eaten with a pinch of salt. Until very recently there used to be a special annual chestnut market in a local town and of course chestnut wood is used in furniture production, parquet floors and is a useful fuel.

The problem in using chestnuts in the kitchen is the difficulty in removing their shells and inner skin and this is probably the reason why fewer and fewer of the local ladies collect and cook them today. In theory, it is forbidden to pick chestnuts before All Saints' Day unless the tree belongs to you but every year tons are now run over and wasted. Chestnut leaves are often used to wrap goat's cheese in or used to line the cheese platter.

Here's one recipe which is worth doing:

1kg chestnuts, ¼ litre milk, vanilla pod, 100g caster sugar, 4 eggs

Boil the split chestnuts in water for 30minutes and peel...both skins...trying to find the patience!

Poach the cleaned chestnuts in the milk with the vanilla pod for 15 mins.

Crush the chestnuts with a fork.

Separate the yolks from the 4 eggs and mix with the sugar and then add the pureed chestnuts.

Whisk the egg whites and when fluffy fold into the chestnut mixture and pour into a buttered and floured mould.

Bake for 90mins in the oven at 150°c.

Remove from the mould and allow to cool.

Melt 200g cooking chocolate in a bain marie and spread over the cake. Allow to cool in the fridge.

Serve with « crème anglaise » (custard) which is made by mixing 4 egg yolks with 125g caster sugar onto which is poured ½ litre of boiling milk.

Place on the heat for a couple of minutes but do not boil. Cool rapidly and strain to remove any lumps.

Serve a portion of the cake with cold crème anglaise.

Traditionally, in these parts, any cake is divided into the number of persons present, leaving no left-overs... this can be fine, but if it's an English rich fruit Christmas cake, there can be a problem as we found out at our first Christmas here! Chestnut cake is also very filling, so there could be left-overs!

2. « La noix » (Walnuts)

Everyone has access to a walnut tree here. 'A walnut tree takes 100 years to grow, is fully grown for another 100 years and then takes 100 years to grow old and die'. Walnut wood is used by cabinet makers, sculptors and joiners, its bark is used in tanning, dying and in the manufacture of ink.

Beekeepers use the shells for smoking bees and the same shells are useful in lighting fires. A bottle of walnut oil was always to be found on the table in a pay-san's house in our area to flavour food with the salt and pepper. Consuming walnut oil helps to reduce choles-terol and it is the richest of all oils in polyunsaturated fat (higher than olive oil). Used mostly in dressing salads, it is also used to flavour, pancakes, bread and mohjettes...

Shelled walnuts are added to salads and walnut tart with honey is a rich dessert.

Vin de Noyer (Wine from walnut leaves)

Chop 250 grams walnut leaves and add 30g of finely cut bitter orange peel and powdered nutmeg. Pour on 1 litre of alcohol at 90° and leave to macerate for 24 hours. Then add 5 litres red wine and 1 kg sugar. Macerate for a further 15 days or more. Filter and bottle...and drink!

Vin de Noix (Walnut Wine)

Pick 12 young, green walnuts. Test the nuts by pushing a darning needle straight through; if the needle meets a hard casing/shell, you're too late and you'll have to wait until next year!

To the 12 nuts, cut into 4, add 1kg of sugar, 1 chopped orange and 1 litre of eau de vie together with 12 litres of red wine. Leave to macerate 3 months before decanting. There will be a thick, black deposit which will stain your hands. In fact all parts of the walnut tree are perfumed and will stain skin easily.

3. L'Ortie (Nettles)

Not a detestable weed but a very useful plant. You can make wonderful liquid compost from nettles and no end of health and medicinal products from shampoo, to body oil and face masks and as a cure for intestinal problems.

It is also a wonderful vegetable! It is used chopped in an omelette, likewise in a quiche, in desserts, soufflé's and even is made into a syrup and a refreshing drink. Sue, my wife, often makes nettle soup and nettle shortbread.

«Soupe d'ortie»

Pick a large bowlful of nettle tops – just the small, young leaves (wear gloves!). Chop two onions and gently fry in oil; add 2/3 of the nettles and stir gently.

Add a couple of sliced carrots, a couple of sliced courgettes or a stick of celery and two sliced medium-sized potatoes and fry for a few minutes, stirring.

Add 1,5 litres water, salt and bring to the boil. Simmer for 20 minutes.

Put the soup through a blender. Then add the rest of the uncooked nettles and blend once more. Taste and adjust the seasoning. You may wish to add a little milk or cream. « Très bon »!

«Sablés à l'ortie»

To a bowlful of dried nettle shoots which you have rendered as near to a powder as you have been able, mix with 300g flour, 200g sugar and 200g soft butter. Work the mixture lightly with your fingertips and roll out the pastry. Cut into desired shapes and bake at 180°c for 15 minutes.

The biscuits can be covered by a mixture of chocolate and finely chopped fresh mint prepared in a bain-marie if you wish.

4. « Beignets de Sureau » (Elderflower Fritters)

Very simple, this. Pick healthy-looking elderflowers (or acacia flowers) and shake free of any insects.

Make a normal pancake mix and dip the flower heads in the mixture, holding them by the green stalks. Fry in hot oil and serve sprinkled with sugar. Dead easy and a lovely, different snack for « le goûter »

5. « Confiture 'gratte-cul' » Rosehip Jam

Collect 700 grams of wild rose hips and empty each one of its seeds and 'itching powder' (gratte-cul means 'scratch bottom'!).

Marinate the rosehip shells in white wine for 1 week and then place them in a jam pan and cook very slowly for about 1 hour.

Mince the shells and add the juice of a lemon.

Weigh the pureed shells and add the same weight of sugar.

Cook for half an hour.

It's worth the effort!

6. « Les champignons » (Mushrooms)

A panful of freshly cooked mushrooms, prepared in the simplest manner, gives-off such a wonderful odour and they are so wonderful to eat! – no wonder that the locals won't share their favourite hunting grounds and play hide-and-seek in the forest with anyone who tries to follow them!

Every year, little rose field mushrooms appear on our lawn and sometimes pieds bleus, in the lane outside the house parasol mushrooms appear but in the woods, morrels, chanterelles, trompettes de la mort, pieds de mouton and the wonderful cèpes...

Little button mushrooms are good prepared with a fricasée of snails, trompettes de la mort (black chanterelles) are excellent soaked in cognac and then added to the pâté at Piggy-killing time, chanterelles are particularly good when gently fried with scallops (« coquilles St Jacques ») in a cream sauce but the best way to eat any mushrooms quite honestly is just to fry them gently in a little butter with a hint of garlic. Add a little cream if you're feeling greedy and sprinkle chopped parley on before serving on a slice of toast, or with a fried egg, or an omelette... The best free food possible!

17

« Autour du four »
(Around the Bread Oven)

Every hamlet in our commune still has one or more stone-built ovens, lined with bricks – often free-standing like the one opposite our house or incorporated into a house or boundary wall. Originally they were lit once a week and they provided bread for the needs all of the inhabitants for the coming week.

Bundles of brushwood and thicker faggots were set on fire inside the oven and the door left open (normally there is no other exit for the smoke to get out). Further wood was added (two, three or four more bundles of faggots) until the desired temperature was reached.

There was never a thermometer but an experieced oven operator would throw in a handful of dry flour from time to time in order to judge the temperature by the way the flour burned!

Once the oven was hot enough, the glowing embers were dragged out, or more usually, pushed to the sides to make way for the proved dough. Loaves were much larger than today as that helped the bread to stay fresh longer – not the « baguettes » of today which bought in the morning become stale by lunchtime. Bread was the staple diet for all members of the large families in times gone by.

Bread needs a high temperature to bake – as does the local « Tourteau Fromager ». This is a round, black-domed cake/loaf made with fresh goat's cheese. A very popular, traditional thing to eat at apéritif time with a glass of pineau. It has a delicate flavour – not at all cheesey – moist and soft in texture. Some people don't appreciate the burnt flavour of the blackened top and leave it aside but it makes a change from crisps and peanuts.

« Fromager »

To make, you need a 15cm diameter special bowl (which you can find in all the « brocante » or antique shops around). This is lined with a pastry made from flour, butter, an egg yolk, a little water and a pinch of salt. To this is added a filling of 250grams of drained, fresh goat's cheese into which has been stirred 4 beaten egg yolks, 125 grams sugar, 2 tbs milk, 2 tbs of potato flour and a pinch of salt and the beaten egg whites folded-in together with a shot of brandy (optional).

The bowl is then placed in the centre of the oven at 180°c for 50 minutes. You don't put it in with your arm of course but on a flat, long-armed peel. The « tourteau » is ready when its top has blackened.

After the bread and tourteaux have been baked, you can then cook your stuffed tomatoes, grillons and terrines or your roast pork, sausages, quiches, pizzas or fruit tarts. All of the ladies here pride themselves in serving-up straight-forward pastry bottoms covered with a variety of fruits – especially plums; « Mirabelles » are small plums, full of flavour; then there are greengages and golden gages (« reines-claudes ») red plums and purple plums – large and small (the small ones are known locally as « couilles du pape » (Pope's balls as they are purple and elongated somewhat!)

Another popular dessert is called a « **Clafoutis** » (a sort of fruity custard pie). It's interesting that the French don't make fruit pies with a pastry topping. To make a clafoutis you need to mix two eggs with 5tbsps of sugar. Add 60g of melted butter and then 3 large spoonfuls of self-raising flour, a few drop of vanilla essence and a pinch of salt. Mix the above with a little milk and add a packet of baking powder and stir-in plums, cherries or finely sliced apples and pour into the oven dish. Lay a few knobs of butter on the surface and bake for about 30mins.

Different again is « **Tarte fromagère** » for which you will require 5 eggs, 250g sugar, baking powder, 3 tbs of flour, vanilla essence, 500g of « fromage blanc » which resembles quark/curd-cheese/yoghurt but is not grainy like cottage cheese, and a pastry base. Traditionally, in this area, goat's cheese is used but it is also possible to use cheese made from cow's milk or even a mixture of cow's and goat's. (You need to decide if you like the distinctive billygoat taste which can easily be detected in the finished product!) Mix the egg yolks with the sugar thoroughly and then add the fromage blanc (40% fat content) and continue mixing. Whisk the egg whites until snowy peaks are achieved and then fold carefully into the mixture before placing in the pastry case lining the oven dish/tin. Bake for 50 or 60 minutes.

Similar to this is « **Tarte au chèvre** » where a mixture made from 2 fresh goat's cheeses, 3 eggs and fresh cream is poured onto sorrel or lettuce leaves placed on a pastry base in a tart dish and into which some grated hard cheese and flaked almonds are also added. Bake for 30 mins.

The « **Broyé du Poitou** » is this area's answer to short-bread. It is considered such an important biscuit-like dessert that it used to be blessed by the priest at the end of Mass in days gone by. To make, take 500g of flour, 250g of sugar, 250g of butter, 1 egg yolk and a pinch of salt. Mix together and spread out on an oven tray. You can add a few drops of 'goûte' or brandy and a few roasted almonds on the top if you wish or decorate it with a fork. Bake for 30 minutes. The broyé is not cut but traditionally broken by hitting it hard to smash it into pieces.

« Grimolles »

Finally, here is a simple but different local dessert. Make a thickish sweet pancake batter and pour it onto large cabbage leaves which are then placed in the oven. Once cooked, you can peel the pancake off the cabbage leaf or eat the leaf with the pancake! Often, sliced apples are added to the mixture and the resulting sweet eaten with a bowl of cider...

Conclusion?

Food cooked on the hot brick tiles of a bread oven, perfumed by the lingering odour of burning wood really is a treat, and what could be more pleasurable to a would-be « paysan » than to sit in the open-air around the oven with his neighbours, tasting such a variety of savoury and sweet dishes made from local ingredients hot out of the oven and washed down with glasses of wine or pineau? Pity the poor town dweller – and the Deputy Head...! Moving to France might just have been a good idea...

Translation of French Phrases Used in the First Part of the Book

1. *The Quandry*

une maison secondaire – a holiday home

pied à terre – a base

un héritage – an inheritance

vivre à la campagne – living in the countryside

le paysage – the landscape

le doux climat – gentle climate

quelqu'un dans la famille – a family member

la terre, c'est la richesse – land is wealthiness

et la richesse n'a pas de prix – and the value of such
    wealth cannot be measured in monetary terms

servez-vous, faites comme vous voulez – help
    yourselves, do as you wish

Agence immobilière – Estate Agent

Je vais vous montrer quelque chose – I'll show you
    something

un sous-table – an under the table payment

2. *The Dream House*

potager – vegetable garden

l'oeil du bac – the 'eye of the sink'

ça fait du vin qui rend fou – it makes wine that drives you mad

Fête du four – oven party

se cacher dans un lieu perdu – to hide in the middle of nowhere

vin de la vigne – basic, homemade wine

Les gens du Nord – Northeners

ils sont fous ces anglais – the English are crackers

3. *A Banquet?*

J'ai tout le nécessaire – I've brought everything I need

A local meal, one from where we live

plat de résistance – the main dish

Ca ne fait rien si elle n'aime pas le poulet; il y a du lapin si elle préfère – It doesn't matter if you doen't like chicken; there's some rabbit if she prefers.

Non, pas de problème, elle aime bien le poulet, merci Madame. – No, there's no problem, she likes chicken Madame.

Petit bonhomme – little chap

4. *The Slate and the Serviette*

La rentrée – the beginning of the school year

La Toussaint – All Saint's Day

Comment tu t'appelles? – what's your name.

5. *The « Kleenex » Teacher*

Il faut les déguster sans les pieds – you don't eat the
stalks

un chasseur de champignons – a mushroom hunter/
gatherer

avoir beaucoup de pain sur la planche – to be faced with
a hard task (to be faced with a lot of bread)

un bain linguistique – language immersion

solfège – sol-fa (music theory)

Conseil de Classe – Class Council

un trou perdu – a 'hole' in the middle of nowhere

la France profonde – in the depths of the French
countryside

un coup de rouge – a shot/glass of red wine

6. *Back to the Land*

le programme – the syllabus

Service viticole, j'écoute – Winemaking Department, I'm
listening to you

8. *Monsieur le proviseur and Monsieur le président*

C'est moi qui vous a salué en premier; vous m'avez
   simplement répondu – It was I whould greeted you
   first; you then replied to my greeting.

Nous trouvons pour M Holding et nous condamnons
   l'état – we find Mr Holding to be in the Right and we
   condemn the State.

9. *Pigs, Pineau and Planing*

Voilà, c'est fait – there, that's done.

La paperasse – (overwhelming) paperwork

Cuisine de cochon – cooking and preserving pork-based
   dishes

bistouille – a shot of spirits with a morning coffee

Quelque chose d'util – something that could come in
   handy

APPENDICES

Les Holding : « Nous sommes là pour nous intégrer ».

Le Mellois, c'est leur tasse de thé

**The Mellois Region is their cup of tea
(translated from French)**
A pioneering English family moves into Lorigné. A new breed of inhabitants.

The Holdings: « We are here to integrate »

We are not political refugees. Garry, in his forties and all smiles hasn't left his British humour behind. He and his wife, Susan, have decided to settle in France before Margaret Thatcher sows further turmoil in the country. The couple landed with their three children Natalie, Justin and Richard together with their Border Collie in the deep South of our region at « Le Sauvage » in the commune of

Lorigné on 22nd December last (1989). They are of the mettle to go as far as Tasmania, if they had to.

Susan makes us think of Petula Clark: we expect to see a covered waggon under the barn. A rustic house with a few hens, with Molly the dog looking on and the essential tackle of odds and ends for pioneers. We warm ourselves with a cup of milky tea: mid-April can be chilly. Shetland sweaters are still necessary. « Some of our friends think we are brave, others think we are foolish – but all of them envy us.»

Garry gave up his position as Deputy Head of a Secondary School in the Border Country of County Durham, with its annual salary of 250,000 francs, with no regrets in order to participate in the European adventure for the salary of a supply teacher. Susan is a language assistant in Melle. « You need French nationality to work for the Education Nationale but to be naturalized you need to work for at least two years. » The Holding couple are ready to put up with this vicious circle hoping that the Europe of 1992 will recognise qualifications from different member countries. But Garry feels ready to do something different: why not combine teaching and farming? A professional potpourri – so long as there aren't too many administrative problems.

Susan wants to buy a cow. « The land is fertile here and we like tilling the soil » says Garry who wants to settle in Lorigné, France. « We have come to integrate but we don't want the area to become an English enclave as in the Périgord. No little England here » say the couple who have fled from their compatriots. Susan drives around the country lanes in her 22 year old 2CV blending into the countryside. The baker delivers the daily baguette together with the newspaper. With a French sparkle in their eyes, the Holdings are full of excitement...

LE CHOIX DE LA VIE

RÉCIT Handicapé mental, il a toujours vécu chez les autres. Après douze ans de bonheur, une tragédie fragilise de nouveau sa vie.

MOI, BERNARD, et ma famille formidable

« **La Vie's** » **Chosen Article:** Mentally handicapped, he's always lived in foster families. After twelve years of happiness, a tragedy perturbs his life once more.
(Translated from French)

Me, Bernard, and my wonderful family

« Le Sauvage » is aptly named with its ochre-coloured stone houses, hidden amongst chestnut forests and wild greenery. For Bernard Lamoureux, this hamlet in the commune of Lorigné in Deux-Sèvres, mid-way between Niort and Limoges, is actually paradise. Paradise lost and then found again after a tragedy which will make a lasting impression on him.

When Stéphanie died, Bernard had already been living in other peoples' homes for many years. Mentally handicapped and having lost contact with his parents, brothers and sister, he's always lived in foster families. Three years in one, ten in another He was 34 when he joined the Holding family – a couple with British origins, settled in France since 1990. Garry, an ex-music teacher from the UK now teaches English in Civray 6th form College. Suzanne, a warm and generous person, convinced that she can make a difference to the lives of the needy in our society, became a foster parent. Between 1995 and 2007 Suzanne and Garry looked after Bernard in their home. They fed him and cared for all his needs, giving him stability. Garry Holding hates it when anyone calls Bernard « handicapped ». « *He's intellectually limited* » points-out Garry « *but he has qualities which others don't possess* ». In truth, Bernard's suntanned face and large soft eyes belie nothing of the problems he might have. But Bernard does need to be closely supervised, stimulated and valued at all times. So, after a few fruitless periods in Occupational Therapy Centres, Bernard, a lover of the great outdoors, now spends his time gardening and doing odd jobs, He can't cope with repetitive tasks, so on the two hectares of land, with cow pigs and vegetable garden, he finds his place and stays twelve years at Le Sauvage. He sees the couple's children grow and participates fully in helping to rebuild the ruined farm buildngs. Today, the home is magnificently restored.

But happy times come to an end. At the age of 60 the Holdings justifiably wish to retire. They now seek the freedom they couldn't enjoy for so many years. During all that time, if they wanted some time off, they were obliged to find a temporary solution for Bernard. « *I was worn out* » recounts Suzanne, now 62, with her little Jane Birkin accent. « *This job is very demanding.* » But what would become of their protégé? Another foster family had to be found. « *The slightest change perturbs him greatly* » continues Suzanne. « *We spent two years getting him ready.* » She consults her diary, which she always keeps up to date, on the large kitchen table and describes the first time they met up with Andrée and Gérard Mitaine, the new foster family appointed by the County Council. At the age when the Holdings want to retire, the Mitaines apply to become a foster family...Bernard moves in with them in February 2007. The couple are authorised to look after two handicapped adults and they already have Stéphanie, aged 24, who is very handicapped.

Then on the morning of 22 August 2007, a shocking event. Bernard finds the lifeless body of Stéphanie in the Mitaine's bathroom. The ideal culprit, he is arrested and accused of murder, until Andrée Mitaine admits to having regularly bullied and mistreated Stéphanie. Repeated beatings and untreated wounds had led to her death. The Holdings heard about the tragedy on the local televised news. « *They were saying that Bernard was perhaps guilty and we were refused all information. The Gendarmes, Social Services and the Judicial Authorities told us it was none of our business* »

Very quickly, Bernard was released but then sent to a psychiatric hospital. In fact, the Authorities didn't know what to do with him. According to his legal guardian service, Bernard was a dangerous person and Social Services clearly stated that no foster family would now be willing to look after him after what had happened. « *Bernard in a psychiatric hospital* » roars Garry, two years after the event. « *In no way should he have been there; he* constantly needs reassurance, to be closely cared-for and to feel valued. He's incapable of living locked-up and becomes agressive when too restricted. » Luckily, the lawyer appointed to Bernard's case, Marc Boizard, was very supportive and even accused the psychiatric hospital of illegally retaining a person against their will. « Had he remained locked-up, he would have died » confirmed Maître Boizard.

Even before Bernard was found to be innocent, the Holdings offered to have him back, and after two months of combatting with the authorities he was allowed to return to Le Sauvage. Slowly but surely Bernard is finding his equilibrium once more. Today, just for him and at the age of 62, Suzanne is applying to become a foster family once more. She also knows that from henceforth she can count on the support of Bernard's brother who has since become his legal guardian and who occasionally has him stay – as indeed do other newly re-found members of Bernard's family. It has now become a priority for Garry and Suzanne to find a new foster family for Bernard – someone with the patience and the willingness to accept him how he is; with a garden too « but we're in no rush » Suzanne says reassuringly to Bernard.

Seated at the table on the patio of their lovely house, Bernard listens, pensively. On the 18 June – the day the trial opens in Parthenay for Andrée and Gérard Mitaine, he will have to confront them on the witness stand, alone; he who feels threatened for the slightest reason. « *When he doesn't understand what's happening to him his behaviour can be very unpredictable* » says his lawyer, concerned. The Holdings will be in court to help him through the ordeal; supporting him one more time.

A Witness called Bernard (From the « La Vie » website) (Translated from French)

Court Case. A 12-year prison service for Andrée Mitaine was the verdict of the Parthenay Assizes for having caused the death of Stéphanie, a young mentally handiapped woman in August 2007. How did Bernard, the other handicapped person looked after by Madame Mitaine, fare through two days of the court case?

Everyone foresaw it, and especially Garry and Suzanne Holding, his foster family. He had been particularly nervous for two days preceding the trial as being summoned to testify during the case was inevitably going to be particularly anxious time for Bernard. Anxiety could be detected as soon as he arrived in court – the Gendarmes, the juges in their black and red robes and the security measures to be gone through. And then once in the court room, he sees, for the first time since the day of the tragic event, Andrée Mitaine seated in the dock.

Convoked to be present at 9,00am, he is told to go away and to return at four thirty to appear before the court; 7 additional hours of waiting and worrying. Once the dreaded moment does arrive, he manages to say, in a sqeuaky voice, that he is called Bernard and that he lives with Garry and Suzanne. Then the sobbing starts and the judge asks « are you related to the accused? ». He finds it impossible to reply and breaks down. The judge remains calm and tries to reassure him but Bernard doesn't understand the question. Garry Holding is authorised to stand next to him at the bar and to explain to the court that Bernard is under legal guardianship – something which, visibly, the Judge and his counsellors were unaware of and who immediately refer to the statute book to establish what procedure to follow.

The interrogation continues « *Did you see Madame Mitaine hit Stéphanie?* » the judge asks. Bernard replies in a clear voice « *It was me who found Stéphanie and I pulled her out of the bath, she was very cold. Mr G (her legal guardian at that time) didn't do his job properly, that's all.* » And that would be all: no questions asked by the Prosecutor General or by the Accusation or Defence lawyers.

Bernard's statement, then, served no great purpose other than to publicly display his psychological vulnerability and to obtain feelings of sympathy from the public gallery. In any case the Court had already received enough evidence to condemn Andrée Mitaine and to send her down for twelve years. Her husband, accused of failing to assist a person in danger, received a suspended sentence of three years.

Comment by Jean Marc Boizard

We know of Bernard's case through having been his lawyers; a case which is emblematic for the weaker amongst us – the mentally handicapped who have difficulty in obtaining the slightest respect in our society.

Unfortunately, the judicial system already exudes so much contempt towards the Accused that the importance of underlining the idea of 'innocent until proven guilty' is paramount in the rôle of a lawyer.

Bernard was viewed as being the ideal culprit from the very beginning and this would have been the easy and perfect solution for all concerned. Incarcerated in a psychiatric hospital, he was submitted to constraints and to be a victim to anxious fears which could have him rendered very violent indeed. Unscrupulous administrators could even have made him admit to things he was innocent of.

We feel ourselves particularly fortunate to have been at his side from the very beginning of the affair and to support the theory that he had killed no one; to have been able show our trust in him and to be able to cope with his difficulties in communicating and his way of interpreting facts.

The Holdings were immediately willing to take him back, inspite of the fact that the County Council Social Services had branded him as being a dangerous murderer. His case is not closed, however, and we do not know if he will continue to be vigorously pursued with a view to prosecution, accused of also having slapped the young girl once himself.

Obliging him to appear as a witness was an ordeal from which it would have been very reasonably spared. His weeping at the bar demonstrated that he was being inflicted an unneccessary torture.

Yours, Avocatlantique.com

Postscript

Bernard was pursued and was summoned to appear at the Regional County Court (Tribunal de Grande Instance). His new foster family, quite rightly I believe, chose not to inform him and despite vigorous pleading by his lawyer on the grounds of diminished responsibility due to his handicap - «svp laissez le pauvre bonhomme tranquille » (please leave the poor chap alone), he received a two-year suspended sentence and was deprived of his civil rights. He already had no civil rights, due to his handicap...